C000053818

RUNNING BRITAIN

The final leg of the world's first ever
length of Britain triathlon

By Sean Conway

MORE BOOKS BY SEAN

Land's End to John O'Groats
Cycling the Earth
Hell and High Water

Running Britain
Copyright © Sean Conway 2018
www.SeanConway.com

Sean Conway has asserted his right to be identified as the author
of this Work in accordance with the Copyright, Design and Patent
Act 1988

First published in 2018

Mortimer Lion Publishing
www.MortimerLion.co.uk

Cover Design © Sophie Adams
www.sophieadamsdesign.com

Edited by Liz Marvin

ISBN 978-0-9574497-4-9

If you read this book you are entering into a binding contract to
make the most of this wonderful island we live on, and to keep
on running

To future Mrs Conway.
Who I eventually found while riding my bike in the Lake District.
Here's to many more adventures to come.

Contents

My life on my back for 6 weeks on the road

Prologue

'Good morning ladies and gentlemen, we have now reached Inverness where this bus terminates. I hope you had a good night's rest and do have a safe onward journey.'

Bollocks did I have a good night's rest. Of course not! A 15-hour overnight bus where the seats only move back about 5cm – why they even bothered designing that – certainly wasn't a good start to my epic run.

It was 9th August 2014, and I had decided to run the length of Britain – John O'Groats to Land's End. Back in 2008, I'd cycled from Land's End to John O'Groats. I did it because I wanted to explore Britain and I didn't have any money to go on holiday. It wasn't an endurance challenge particularly – I didn't ever cycle more than 60 miles a day and I even stopped on the way to climb Ben Nevis. It was an awesome trip though, and something I think anyone could do if you like cycling. Then in 2013 I became the first person to swim from Land's End to John O'Groats, so if I could do this run, I would be the first person in history to complete a length of Britain triathlon – which sounded kind of nuts whenever I said it out loud.

The only minor hurdle was that, despite my adventure CV not looking too bad in some ways, the one thing I had never really got into was running. It was my Achilles heel – literally. I tore my Achilles heel when I was a teenager. And so running was never my thing – even though my heel is now completely, um, healed. I did like the idea of running, though. You can do it all year round, you only ever have to carry a pair of trainers and (I've been reliably informed) once you get past the initial few weeks it's rather pleasant. It's just those first few weeks – I want to skip them and go straight to the good stuff.

I was looking forward to the run particularly, because I was doing this one for the adventure. There were no sponsors, no records, no planned route or anything. I was being just like Forrest Gump in the film: 'I just wanted to go for a run'. In fact, to inspire me even more (and pre-empt all those imaginative people who would most likely shout 'Run, Forrest!' at me), I had even managed to source a Bubba Gump Shrimp Trading Co. red cap like the one Tom Hanks wears in the film.

This was hopefully going to be one hell of a Great British adventure and I couldn't wait to start it. Just one more train and a bus to John O'Groats. The next six weeks on the road were sure to be epic. I couldn't wait.

'Good morning ladies and gentleman, we have now reached London Victoria where this bus terminates. I hope you had a good night's rest and do have a safe onward journey.'

I hobbled off the bus trying not to bend my leg as shafts of pain pulsated through my knee, my leg brace not working at all. The lady next to me had a copy of *The Sun* newspaper and there, taking up half of page 27, was the headline: 'SELFIE HARM – SEAN KO'd BY SELFIE DURING FINAL LEG OF GB TRIATHLON'

I tried not to make eye contact in case she recognized me; my Forrest Gump-like beard was a dead giveaway. My run had not gone to plan at all. Just days into the adventure I was doing a video diary while running and I tripped on a rock and injured my knee – hence the 'SELFIE HARM' headline, which was not only incredibly embarrassing but also a little insensitive to people who actually have problems with self-harm, but hey, that's Rupert Murdoch for you. I knew I shouldn't have put the video on YouTube though, it was my own fault really. The only plus side was that the extra publicity did help me raise more money for The British Heart Foundation, my chosen charity for the run. I tried not to think about it as, somehow, even thinking seemed to cause pain in my knee.

Maybe I just wasn't cut out for running. It would be weeks before I'd know the extent of my injury, following doctors' examinations and MRI scans. The reality was that there was a good chance I may have done irreparable damage, thus ending any possibility of me completing my length of Britain triathlon. That made me incredibly sad, the kind of sad that has no light at the end of the suffocating, oxygen deficient tunnel.

Seven months later . . . 'Screw it. Let's do it!' I said to my adventure mascot, Little Flying Cow, who's actually a bull, as I lay on my bed watching my fire burning, gently rocking from side to side. It's at this point I should mention that I live on a 1932 Second World War gunboat and not in a hammock, although that would be cool, and yes, I do have a fireplace in my bedroom.

My 'selfie fail' continued to haunt me whenever I met people for the first time. 'Are you the guy who got injured taking a selfie?' They'd ask, and then burst out laughing. All that hard work swimming the length of Britain forgotten, and replaced by the daftest of accidents. My parents are so proud!

Luckily the doctor said it was just a bruised bone and I took the next four months to let it heal. By February I'd managed a few runs, but nothing serious. I had no idea whether running the length of Britain was still possible for me. In the back of my mind I still wondered if I was cut out for running. But, despite my doubts, I figured I'd give it one more go. I decided to watch *Forrest Gump* again to fuel my excitement.

To add to my excitement, I also got an email from Discovery Channel* saying they wanted to send a film crew to follow my run. If that wasn't enough pressure not to get injured then nothing would be. It was all or nothing now. No turning back.

---

* I decided from the outset not to include the filming side of my run in this book for no other reason than it didn't impact in any way on the run and I wanted to get across what it was like to run for 6 weeks unsupported. Although there was a film crew, they did not in any way help me at all during the run and were very much a fly on the wall as I trundled down Britain. Discovery Channel did a great job with the documentary and it was watched all over the world – something I am very proud of.

Back at John O'Groats, ready for my second attempt

Chapter 1 – My Old Friend John

Standing at the edge of the cliff as if it were thinking about jumping, stood the old John O'Groats House Hotel. It used to be covered in graffiti and have a real *Trainspotting* feel to it. However, it had recently been given a new lick of paint, as well as a fancy colourful Scandinavian-like wooden extension to the side. When I arrived on a windy March morning, the café (which is now 'PROUD TO SERVE STARBUCKS') was busy and a coachload of Japanese tourists were battling strong winds to take photos by the famous sign (installed by the same company who put up the other one at Land's End in the 1960s), with *we took an eight-hour bus ride for this?* looks on their faces.

Despite the somewhat disappointing, touristy feel to the place, I bloody loved this remote corner of Scotland. Arriving back here, at the top of mainland Britain, brought with it a strange sense of déjà vu. This was the fourth time I'd travelled up here. This time I'd flown, and the previous time was the terrible bus journey, but before that I had swum here and the first time I ever went to John O'Groats I arrived on a bike.

This time I was doing it the other way around, heading south and finishing at Land's End for the first time – selfies notwithstanding. I'd decided to do it this way round partly because I liked the idea of starting out in the wildest part of the country on my own, with the route heading through more populated areas as I went south. And for the more practical reason that this early in the year I was unlikely to be troubled by the famous Scottish midges. Sure, it would be colder, but I didn't think it would be too bad . . . Oh, and of course because running this way means it's all downhill, right? I wondered how many people would tell me that over the next six weeks. I really couldn't wait to hear that over and over again!

'Sean! Sean! You're back. What are you doing this time?' A gentleman came over to me with a camera in his hand. I recognized him as the curio shop owner down by the harbour, but I couldn't remember his name. I'm awful with names and I hate myself for it. It's always my New Year's resolution to remember people's names, and I've even done a memory course to help me, but in 33 years I've still not found a cure.

Normally my go-to generic name is 'mate', but in Scotland they don't say mate, it's 'pal'. Mate or pal? Mate or pal? My brain in that split second didn't know which to go for.

'Hello Mal,' Dammit! I really needed to find out his name. (It was Walter.)

'I'm going to do the run this time,' I continued quickly, hoping he didn't hear me calling him Mal.

'Without taking a selfie, right?' he said, with a big grin. Great. I really was never going to live that stupid selfie down. My gravestone will read: 'Sean Conway. Fairly competent at many things in life but taking selfies was not one of them. RIP.'

'Come down to my shop, I have something to show you.'

I followed him down the steps and into the curio shop where he took me to a rack of postcards, one of the ones that you can spin around. He spun it half a revolution then looked at me. I wasn't quite sure what he was showing me. I looked at the postcards and then back at him.

'Can't you see it?' he asked excitedly.

Dammit. I wasn't prepared for a game of hide-and-seek. I just wanted to start my run. I looked closer and suddenly I saw it. There, fifth row down, was a postcard of me, in my wetsuit, from when I finished my length of Britain swim.

'No way! You have a postcard of me! That's amazing.'

'Here you go Sean, you can have one.'

He took a single postcard out of the huge pile and gave it to me.

'Are you sure?'

'Yes of course. I have loads.'

'Because no one buys them.' I joked.

There was an awkward silence. This was obviously true. How embarrassing. I didn't care though. I had a postcard of me and I can therefore die happy with the endnote to my gravestone: 'But he did have a postcard'.

The John O'Groats sign is the 'official' start for a length of Britain attempt, and most people think of it as the most north-easterly tip of Britain. However, if you look on the map there is a small headland off to the east called Duncansby Head. This is where I was going start my run. The track ends at the top of some pretty dramatic cliffs that feel a world away from the commercial 'attraction' of John O'Groats. It was a three-mile round trip but I felt it was worth it to officially start the run away from the tourists and capitalist coffee, alone on the cliffs.

It took me no time at all to get to the lighthouse at the end of the road. The wind was gusting so hard I very nearly lost my Bubba Gump hat. I got as close to the cliffs as possible before turning my tracker on to officially start the run. I had a SPOT tracker which was a palm sized device that I clipped onto the top of my backpack. It would send a signal up to a satellite every 2 minutes which would update my website of my whereabouts. I knew quite a few people, mostly my friends and family would be waiting and watching online for me to start, and then give me loads of advice from the comfort of their armchairs that I was going the wrong way I bet. Anyhow, it was great to be able to share my adventure with anyone who cared to watch a smelly, hairy chap run 1,000 miles the length of Britain.

With the tracker flashing away I climbed up onto the top of the fence, pretended to be Leonardo Di Caprio in *Titanic*, took a quick photo of some cliffs and then turned around.

'This is it Little Flying Cow. Let's smash it,' I shouted to my adventure mascot and started sprinting down the hill as fast as my little legs could take me. I felt strong and in no time at all I was a few hundred metres away from the cliff heading back towards John O'Groats.

I decided to try taking a short cut along the cliffs but within minutes I was completely lost. Honestly! How hard can it be? Keep the sea on your right. Eventually after some subtle trespassing and rock scrambling over very slippery seaweed I was back in the car park heading towards the sign, as I figured I should still get a photo by the sign seeing as that's what everyone else does. You know, when in Rome. . .

All of a sudden the challenge became real, and my mind began to wander. I felt nervous for the first time. What if I got injured again? I was stronger but I had no idea how my knee would cope. The closer I got to the sign the faster my heart raced. If there was ever a time where I needed to get my act together, it was now. This was it. Running Britain was about to . . .

'Woooo!!! Partaaaayyyyyy!!!' a chorus of screaming erupted to my right. My daydream was shattered by a gaggle of girls, dressed to the nines, giggling and screaming. Pouring out of a bus, they ran/galloped/hobbled over the small stones all the way up to the sign. Was this really happening? I'd just been beaten to the sign by what looked like some sort of hen do. Who comes to John O'Groats for their hen party? I thought that if you combined the material of all 15 girls' dresses, you'd barely make one suitable dress. Hmm, I seemed to have become a very grumpy old man. I glanced around. The few onlookers didn't even raise a smile. Maybe this was a normal thing for this part of the world.

I looked back, and as quickly as they arrived they were all giggling and hobbling back to the bus in their ridiculous stilettoes. There was one more obligatory 'WOOP!' and the bus sped off around the corner. The newfound quiet was punctuated by a 'splat' sound. A seagull had shat on the pavement right next to me. All I could think about was if that turd had landed on my head because I had waited for the girly bus party to leave I would have been rather annoyed.

Right, back to the task at hand, running 1,000 miles – the length of Britain. Now this really was it. I very undramatically went to the sign, touched it and ran off, round the front of the hotel and carried on along the coastal path.

The path was often a river with all the rain

Chapter 2 – The Long Way Round

With any challenge or adventurous undertaking, getting to the start line can feel much harder than the journey itself. Well, except maybe when I swam Britain; that was significantly tougher than the preparation, although I'm pretty sure I wrote a similar sentence about getting to the start line in the book about that too.

Of all the worries in preparing for this run, one of the more annoying issue was with my 'second home', my trusty red 20 year-old Land Rover Defender called Mana. She had a full-length bed in the back, so when I was away from home I could sleep in the back of her; for example, outside a school before doing a talk in assembly the following morning. Something I'd hopefully never have to explain to the police. I'm still not sure if you're actually allowed to sleep in your car, but it is way easier than getting up at 5am and battling rush hour. So I'd often take a leisurely drive up the night before, park in a quiet road away from street lights, and have a good sleep.

I've had lots of great adventures with Mana. Apart from providing a mobile hotel room, we've road-tripped to the south of France, spent two weeks parked up in the Alps battling -15 degrees C where everything, including her diesel froze, and once even drove to Spain to collect my friend's desert buggy. Mana and I had formed a special bond and it seemed that she didn't want me to go on this running adventure without her. A few days before I left, she started to leak fuel. I didn't have the time to send her to the garage, so decided I'd leave it until I got back. The problem was potentially 65 litres of diesel spilling onto the road – something I'm pretty sure the council would frown upon ever so slightly. So for the last few days I drove around the block 100 times at full revs trying to use up as much fuel as possible. The engine eventually cut out going around a left-hand corner, which also, as it turned out, meant the brakes didn't work; a pretty nerve-wracking few seconds to say the least. But at least I was now safe in the knowledge I only had about a litre or two in the tank to annoy the council with.

It's amazing how much nonsense we all have to deal with in the humdrum of 'real life'. If you're not careful your brain gets consumed with tasks, chores and worries, like am I going to get arrested by the council for diesel spillage, or what will people think if I don't iron my shirt before work. Real life is hard work, and it's only when you go off and do these, or any adventures, that you realise how much energy and time you've often wasted. I'm not saying that I want to bow out of real life, it certainly has its rewards like community, friends and family, and I certainly couldn't go away for years, but it was a huge weight off my shoulders knowing that for the next 6 weeks I didn't have to worry about taking the bins out on Wednesday night at 11pm because any earlier and next door's cat gets into them. I was essentially having 'real life' detox if you will. As challenging (and at times miserable) as running 1000 miles was likely to be, it would most certainly be worth it in the long run. As long as I didn't get injured again. No more running selfies.

The first major town south of John O'Groats is Inverness. To get there means running along the king cobra of roads, the deadly A9/A99. Many cyclists and few runners have been knocked over on that section. I have been run over once before and wasn't in the mood for it to happen again, so my only other option was to head west for three days, or five days because I'm probably not as fit as I had hoped, before being able to turn south. This would mean I could explore more of the remote areas of northern

Scotland, whilst visiting places I stopped at when I was swimming the length of Britain. I was really looking forward to seeing these small villages again under new circumstances and reminiscing about those tough last weeks of the swim. Nostalgia is nearly my favourite feeling, after the satisfaction of a good Scottish single malt. With any luck I'd be able to have both at the same time. Dream big I say.

After this first bit, well, I didn't really have a route planned. My plan was just to take it day by day. I'd spent quite a lot of time looking at a map of the UK of course (as looking at maps is a fun thing to do), but more to daydream about the remote and beautiful places in Britain I'd be spending time in, rather than actually deciding on a definitive route. I wanted to run off road as much as I could – as it's obviously just much more fun (and safer) to be away from traffic, although I had to balance distance against where I would run. I knew that I wouldn't be able to avoid main roads altogether as more winding routes would add too many miles and put me behind schedule.

I planned to take advantage of some of the country's long distance walking trails, where they went a direction that was helpful to me. The first would be the Great Glen Way, one of my favourite tracks, that would take me to Fort William. Then I'd have the West Highland Way to Glasgow. I was looking forward to the Lake District section, as this is one of my favourite places in England. After Kendal, in Cumbria, and down into the Midlands, there would be canal towpaths that would hopefully be good to run along and help me get some miles under my belt. I already knew all about the Severn Way, as it goes close to where I lived in Worcester, finishing in Bristol. Once I got to the West Country, I was excited about running through remote Dartmoor, and I hoped to be able to finish my journey on the South West Coast Path.

From the outset I always wanted to try and run a marathon a day. It seemed a real challenge but not ridiculous mileage that would remove all adventure from the run. Running just over 26 miles per day, with a 10kg rucksack was far beyond anything I had ever attempted in my life but that notion in itself was my fuel. Would I manage it? I honestly wanted to believe I could, but it seemed a very daunting task indeed.

Right now though, I had only just started and already my poor organizational skills were causing me problems. Not only had I managed to leave John O'Groats after 4pm – meaning that it wasn't long before I was running down quiet back roads in pitch darkness – I'd packed my head torch right at the bottom of my bag. I stopped and emptied everything out on the side of the road, rummaging impatiently amongst my gear to find it. Naturally, being March, it was quite windy and within seconds my camping mat had unfurled and was being blown down the road.

'Bollocks!' I shouted out loud. A few cows in the field to my left looked up as I chased after it. The camping mat was winning the race by a mile and if it hadn't been for a prickly bush snagging it I'd probably have ended up all the way back at John O'Groats.

'I hope it didn't get a puncture,' I said to myself. My mum always used to tell me, 'Talking to oneself is the first sign of madness,' which used to bother me a bit, but now I really don't care. So long as you sound confident, you can get away with it, right? And anyway, sometimes it may *look* like I am talking to myself, but actually I am talking to Little Flying Cow. Which is not the same thing at all.

I reached Dunnet Bay by 8pm and found the only place open, a small inn right on the main road, thus avoiding an annoying detour, and decided that was that for me for the night. I had run 17 miles in a disappointingly slow four hours.

'Hey, aren't you the chap doing the run?' said a man sitting at the bar as I ordered a lasagne and a pint of Guinness. Word does spread quickly in these parts.

'No, I'm an accountant,' I replied cheekily, and immediately regretted it.

'Really? Well there is another chap with a huge beard who is running the length of Britain. You look exactly like him,' he said, turning around, a lot less interested now.

'I'm kidding, I am him!' I said, feeling a bit stupid for making a pretty rubbish joke.

'Ah, OK,' he replied, not looking back. Maybe he thought I was lying. He then fell off his chair while trying to lean over the bar to pour himself his own pint. I did try not to laugh at him, but sadly I couldn't help it and gave a very loud and annoying single 'HA!' The man at the bar recomposed himself and inspected the chair as if to suggest there was something wrong with it. We've all been there.

My head said I should get a room in the pub for the night as I could do with a good sleep after a long week preparing to leave 'real life' behind, which is actually often harder than the journey itself. As they say, getting to the start line is often the hardest thing. That was my head, however, my heart, which generally goes for the harder, albeit more adventurous option, said I should camp on the beach instead. A quick scan of the OS map on my phone suggested there were some great little dunes I could shelter in so, after one more pint for the road – OK, two, I had three pints – I got up to go. Immediately I nearly fell over from stiff knees. I reached out to steady myself, and caught hold of the lamp on the table, sending it crashing to the floor. I quickly composed myself and snuck out the back before the bar lady shouted at me for causing a ruckus, or the man who fell off his bar stool could see me.

To ensure the least amount of pressure on my knees, I had found the world's lightest tent, a beautiful 580g and this was the first time I had ever used it. Most people would have actually tested their gear out beforehand however, as I said before, leaving real life behind took up most of my time. I figured I'd work things out as I went along. That was part of the excitement of it all.

Within seconds of taking it out the bag, my excitement was dramatically reduced when I realized the fabric was practically transparent, and then all but gone when I saw the tent pegs. They were thinner than toothpicks and about four inches long with a little hook at the end – great for yard lawn or hard mud but pretty bloody useless in sand. They were the most ridiculous tent pegs I had ever seen, but they saved me at least 20g.

To make matters even worse, it started to rain. There is always a period of vulnerability while setting up camp. You usually need to open your bag and take out various things which lie all over the place and until you've set up your tent and can get everything into shelter. Which, on this occasion, being my first time and all, took forever.

That night, my stuff got very wet, and it turned out my camping mat did have a small puncture from the prickly bush. I made a mental note to fix it in the morning.

Bang on 9am as usual, somewhere between the now closed inn and Castletown, still a few miles ahead, wasn't ideal for my colon to begin its timely disembarkation of last night's Guinness and lasagne – a rowdy combination as it happens. I had packed toilet paper for 'just in case', because I didn't want a repeat of the dog-carcass-rib-bone incident of 2012 in the middle of the Atacama Desert while I was cycling around the world. In a remote and sparsely populated desert it's relatively easy to pop off the road when you need the loo; it's a little less convenient in the open, treeless landscape of far north Scotland, where there are no bushes and most of the fields are patrolled by cows, very angry killer cows. I grew up in Africa, and lived in game reserves, and I can tell you that a buffalo is not nearly as scary as these darned cows. Also, I was sure that there's a certain element of social unacceptability to crapping in a working farmer's field. So I decided to hold on and head to Castletown, and pray for a hotel that was open where, under the pretence that I'd buy a coffee and/or breakfast, I could make one of their loos out of order.

Luckily Castletown did have a hotel, with coffee, but no breakfast. So after a lovely dose of caffeine followed by a rather below average toilet break, I went over the road to a small off licence to stock up on the day's food. The plan was to get to Thurso for late lunch and then push on a bit until dark.

The off licence was much like most examples of its kind. A whimpering dog was chained up outside and the automatic door wasn't quite calibrated, which resulted in me nearly face-planting into the glass before it sluggishly opened at the last second. Once inside, under fluorescent lights the chaotic shelves were stocked with thousands of products you'd never normally buy, packed as close as possible together in order to fit even more products in - unless of course there was a high local demand for seven types of 99p sponge cakes.

It was tough to judge just how much food to carry on each leg. If I didn't take enough, I risked running out of fuel in the middle of nowhere and would then start breaking down muscle mass, something that in the long run could end my attempt. If I carried too much I'd just be putting extra weight on my knees. You need to multiply the weight you carry by seven and that's the weight your knees take on the downhills. So an extra kilo of food, which is simply a small bottle of water, a pie, a banana and some ham – less than an average meal – would add 7kg of weight to my knees on a downhill. That's more than 10 per cent extra of my body weight my knees would have to deal with.

For the past 15 years my knees have been used to carrying around 66kgs or less. If I carried a 10kg pack, multiplied by seven again, that would add yet another 70kg to my knees, which would be like giving myself a piggyback.

So weight really was a big deal and I had been ruthless in my preparation – to the point of ridiculousness, if I'm totally honest. I had cut my toothbrush in half and I took the little fabric bits off the end of my zips, rendering them almost useless while wearing gloves (I'd only discover later down the line). I shortened the fabric on my backpack straps and decided against a second pair of socks. I've always said the second pair reach dirt saturation within a day anyway, and then they just stink out your bag. So my system is to wash your one pair each night and I then sleep with them on, or wrap them around my thigh so my body heat can dry them overnight. This system does work. I took only one pair of socks when I cycled around the world. I made no friends due to my stench but I saved 200g. Priorities I say!

However, despite all my careful planning, all that consideration about reducing weight went right out the window as I practically emptied the off licence in preparation for the day ahead. I could barely close my backpack.

I got a mile down the road before I really realized I had bought way too much food. I decided to stop, again, and eat half of it.

Less than have an hour later and my usually graceful running style was now more of a fast shuffle, as my belly so full I was too scared to breathe through my mouth in case it gave the contents of my stomach a 'light at the end of the tunnel' escape route. And technically, of course, I was still carrying the weight. All that had happened was that it moved from my backpack to my gut. I guessed that I was probably only burning 300–500kcal per hour and I had eaten at least 1,200 kcal, so I'd probably be in Thurso before I had even digested the food in my stomach, and I still had some left over in my pack. I'm not a religious man but I'm pretty sure that throwing food away wouldn't please the Karma Gods, and at this point in time I didn't want to tempt fate so I hobbled on uncomfortably while continuing to moan about it to every cow that would listen to me.

If you really, really like surfing and don't mind driving a very, very long way then Thurso is the place to come, I've been told. I don't surf. Not for want of trying however. I have done what we all do when we're on holiday in Cornwall and rented a foam surfboard and pee covered used wetsuit and spent hours just trying to paddle out past the first set of breakers. When you eventually do, you have to wait an hour for 'your turn' as other 'proper surfers' take the good waves. Eventually it is your go but you're too bloody cold and tired to even stand up on the board, which inevitably results in falling off immediately and being washing machined in the waves all the way back to shore again. (I even broke a rib by falling back onto my board once.) We still however get back to work on Monday and tell everyone about our 'epic surfing weekend catching some gnarly waves man'.

I have fond memories of Thurso from swimming Britain as this was the point where I was pretty certain it was in the bag. I thought about the few nights I spent here back in 2013 as the crew and I fattened up and got a little tipsy in premature celebrations. I was feeling very nostalgic again. Annoyingly it was too early to have single malt.

As I wandered the streets to get some food someone shouted at me.

'Mate, aren't you the swimmer?' A young chap ran over to me, nearly getting mowed down by a youth speeding around the corner in a beaten-up Renault in the process.

'Yes mate. Although I'm now pretending to be a runner.'

It was nice to still be remembered for the swim. This chap obviously hadn't read about 'Selfie Harm'. We exchanged a few niceties, like you do – 'Horrible weather on the way' and 'Wow, a marathon a day' – before we both went our separate ways, which embarrassingly, after saying goodbye and all, was in fact the same direction, towards Tesco, when for a good minute and a half I was walking about five metres behind him, in silence.

I had a big section ahead of me with potentially no food stops. As it was before Easter, when cafés start opening for the season, most places would still be closed for the winter. So, despite my concerns about carrying too much weight, I needed to stock up for nearly two days, just in case. I was heading towards one of the most uninhabited parts of Europe, north-west Scotland, and I was expecting the landscapes to be pretty desolate

Leaving Thurso gave me the opportunity to deal with my first mountain to run up. OK, it was a hill. Well, no, I lied again, a slope. It was just a gentle slope. Anyway, by the time I reached the top my knees were feeling a tight pain that was way worse than the difficulty of the hill could account for. I hoped it was because most of Tesco being in my rucksack, a scenario that was far preferable than being in pain from a gentle slope. I felt the beginnings of niggling worry growing in the back of my brain.

My route out of Thurso followed the inland back road instead of the main coastal route. It was slightly longer but a lot quieter which allowed me to enjoy the scenery more. And what incredible scenery it was. Hundreds of cotton balls covered the sky occasionally allowing a shaft of light to pierce through, turning the landscape into a magic wonderland for a moment. I became excited – well, a bit obsessed – with these brief moments of beauty. It gave me something to look forward to as the miles slid away underneath my fairly tired legs.

Some seriously windy days in Scotland

Chapter 3 – The Radioactive Runner

I knew they'd be trouble by their rust-bucket of a car, and the way they were driving. The couple sped past me, half in the middle of the road and in about two gears lower than they should be, completely ruining the calm silence I was enjoying. They found a space to pull over about 50 metres ahead of me, jumped out and ran into the road. I thought they were in their early fifties at first, but as they got closer I realised they could have been in their early forties, years of alcohol having taken their toll. That might sound judgy, but it was with some degree of confidence as he was holding a glass full of whisky. I'm sure he was the one driving too.

'We saw you running,' he shouted at me, half spilling his whisky.

He's very observant, I thought.

'Watch it honey, that's the good stuff, remember.'

'Sorry dear.'

They then both stood there staring at me. I guess it was my turn to say something.

'Hi, yes, I am running.'

'We saw you running.'

This is going to be a fun conversation, I thought.

'Where are you heading?'

'Land's End,' I said, keeping it brief.

'World's End, the one in Edinburgh?'

'Obviously, honey. He's not running all the way to Camden Town, London.'

I don't know how many World's End pubs there are in Britain but I was quite impressed they knew the location of two.

'Ha ha. You're right, honey. Obviously. We had a pint there

once didn't we?'

'Yes, we did.'

They then spent the next ten minutes telling me all about the time they had a pint in the World's End, Edinburgh, which resulted in someone wearing the wrong coloured kilt, an orange one apparently, and being punched in the face after a football match between some or another sides that didn't like each other very much.

'Where are you staying tonight? Come stay with us on the hill. We have good whisky.' The last part was said in unison, as if routine: the kind of routine Bonnie and Clyde probably had.

'Thanks,' I replied, 'but I really need to get to the World's End by the end of the week.'

'Aren't you going the wrong way? Edinburgh is the other way.'

'Yeah, but I want to miss the A9 and A99.'

'Oh yes, the bloody A99. We hate the A99 don't we honey?'

'Yes we do. Bloody hate it.'

'Anyway, I really need to get going. Lovely to meet you.'

'You too pal. Say hi to Billy at World's End for us,' they said, even though they hadn't given me their names, thankfully.

I was quite relieved to be running again after my brief encounter with Bonny and Clyde. Any rest longer than ten minutes makes my legs start to seize up and I still didn't have the confidence to stretch while talking to people as I think it always looks a bit weird. What an oversight, really.

By nightfall I had reached the small village of Reay. Annoyingly, there was a little shop that sold everything I needed, which meant I'd carried two kilos of extra food from Tesco for nothing. Oh well. It was time to look for somewhere to sleep.

My maps suggested there was a beach not far away, so I decided to look for a camping spot. The one downside with satellite view on the OS maps app was you were never quite sure whether the photo was taken at low or high tide. Sometimes there is no beach at high tide and you only know when you get there, which can be really annoying if the beach is quite a distance off course. At a mile off my route it wasn't too bad so headed off down a quiet lane. In my fatigued state I had forgotten that I could have just checked the normal OS maps, not the satellite view, to see the high and low tide mark, thus avoiding needless worry.

Twenty minutes later I arrived at the beach and it seemed I was in luck. Although it was small, it looked like I'd have a wide enough ledge above high water to set up camp. You can always tell where the water came up to last by the smoothness of the sand. My camping spot also had enough footprints that looked a few days old to warrant the risk. There was however the small chance it was spring tide, when the water probably did cover my ledge, but I figured if the waves got that close I'd wake up in time.

My tent pegs were never going to work in the sand so instead I had to wrap the line around a stick a few times and then bury it a foot into the sand. This wouldn't hold up in gale force 6 or above, but hopefully that wouldn't happen. With all fingers and toes crossed for not being blown away by the wind, or swept away by the tide, I fell asleep to the sounds of crashing waves off in the distance.

Bollocks. I forgot to fix the puncture in my mat and had to blow it up three times in the night.

'Must remember to fix it at lunchtime,' I said to Little Flying Cow, who was now strapped to the back of my rucksack.

Although I'd only had a broken sleep, I still somehow felt

refreshed. I guarantee it was the sounds of the waves psychologically affecting my mood. The same sleep pattern back home would have most certainly resulted in grumpy Sean.

Packing up in the sand always results in the sodding stuff getting everywhere. There was even sand right at the bottom of my bag even though it had been in my tent all night and not touched the sand. To save weight I was going to leave my pack of baby wipes at home, saving me 200g, but at the last minute I'd decided it was a necessity, as I wasn't sure how many showers I would have. Keeping one's undercarriage clean, and salt and sand free, is important to avoiding chaffing. With the extra sand that had somehow landed up down there I was quite glad I had those little moist pieces of cloth. Also, the eucalyptus ones tingle slightly. You're welcome lads.

All packed up, I started heading back through the dunes to the road. About halfway I saw a yellow sign, partially covered by grass. It looked important. I moved the grass aside to read it:

Radioactive contamination in the form of metallic particles has been found on this beach. The radioactive particles cannot be identified by the human eye.

Members of the public are advised not to remove any objects or materials (including sand, stones & shells) from the beach.

What the . . .? Are they serious? Surely they need a bigger sign, or a gate, or the army to stop people going to the beach? I had sand everywhere, literally everywhere. This was not good. I had basically slept in a huge pile of potentially radioactive powder. Some of which was now in my groin. Worried about landing up with watermelon nadds, I sprinted out of the dunes and back up to the main road to continue west.

The extra weight on my knees the previous day became obvious within minutes. My right knee, the one that had taken the beating during my selfie fail, was really tight. I hadn't really looked after it in these first few days. Ideally I should have been stretching on the side of the road but I had been so caught up in getting the miles in, that marathon a day goal right in the front of my mind, and also if I stopped, I got really cold. Trying to stretch in my tiny coffin tent each night wasn't at all possible either. I just hoped I'd be able to find a good place to stretch, like a pub or something, at lunchtime so sluggishly pushed on.

I was enjoying being in no man's lands, mostly because barely any cars came along this route. Other than a couple in a campervan and a man with a dog that really didn't like me very much – the dog, that is, the man was very pleasant – I didn't see anyone all day. In my previous, doomed attempt at Running Britain I had run this exact route, so I knew a few places where I might be able to get food. Lunch I knew would be at the Melvich Hotel and the good news was that I had taken a short cut before that had saved me at least one-and-a half-miles. It went via a disused bridge, with a sign saying not to cross as it is unstable. This sign however was a lot more noticeable than the radioactive one informing me of my potential untimely death. So were the barricade of wire and the plank of wood I had to jump over in order to get across the bridge. I do feel the radioactive beach should have used the same signage guy as they did here. I really was living on the edge today. The bridge didn't break apart (which would have made this book a lot shorter) but I felt good for saving some much needed miles on the legs. This short cut was also my first real time I'd been off the main road, which was a relief. No matter how quiet the roads were, I could never quite relax – a side effect of getting run over in America when I was cycling round the world. (The full story is in another book of mine, if you want to hear it!).

I was safely over the bridge. I had successfully navigated a clever shortcut and I was feeling pretty smug. The smug gods of doom obviously realized this and, predictably, they immediately got to work to snatch away my smugness as quickly as they could. I reached the Melvich Hotel to find it was still closed for the winter. There was another pub nearby where I was pretty sure I could get lunch, but to get there I had to head one mile back down the part of the road I had cut off. So my 'short-cut' was now going to be about a mile longer, or thereabouts.

Depressed, I hobbled down the road and settled in for a burger and ale, as well as taking the chance to wash my nether regions properly in the men's toilets. I'm pretty sure 'radioactivity' is on the 'will not remove' list on the baby wipes website. I doubted cheap hand sanitizer would be any better but, after a moment weighing up the possible pros and cons, I decided to give it a go.

The pub was pretty empty, so I thought I'd take the opportunity to do some stretching. I found a quiet corner and began a series of poses that should never ever be done in a public place, let alone in a small Scottish pub. Luckily the old man and the Labrador at the bar didn't seem to care, so I continued letting out a few oooohs and aaaahs in between taking sips of ale.

My second task was to tape up my knee. Years ago, I had considered taping to be some sort of hippy nonsense, but fairly recently I worked out that, in fact, it really does work. There's a lot of science in it – far too much to bore you with here – but in essence stretching some parts of the skin will activate the muscles around it. So, if you have a weak glute, tape it and it will start working on its own. It's all very clever.

I needed to tape the inside of my leg, the VMO if you care to know (or vastus medialis oblique if you *really* care to know – I actually had to google that if I'm honest), so that it activated to keep my knee in alignment. My right quad is a bit tight, which pulls my knee off to the outside of my leg. Strong VMOs should keep the kneecap on track and working perfectly. My friend James says that if tape doesn't work then spray WD40 on your knee. As much as that is a joke there is a very small part of me that wants to try it.

Once taped, my final bit of motivation was to write 'SHUT UP KNEE' on the tape. This was inspired by German cyclist Jens Voigt who, after a killer climb on the Tour de France, told journalists that when was tired he just used to shout 'Shut Up Legs'. If it worked for him then hopefully it would work for me too.

Leaving the pub after lunch I really felt like I was in the middle of nowhere. It was a bit like I was on the moon. If the moon had grass, telephone lines and a couple of sheep. Moor, is I guess what the term probably is, which is almost the same word. That thought alone kept my brain busy for at least an hour as I pondered the notion that the word *moor* and *moon* were somehow related.

Off to my left, rolling treeless hills stretched as far as the eye could see, with the Atlantic Ocean (or North Sea, to be honest I'm never quite sure which one it is along this coast) churned away on my right. I realized that there had been a few houses dotted around, but now nothing. Just me, some grass, the ocean and those two sheep in the distance. I felt very alone for the first time.

Less than an hour later and I realized categorically that writing 'Shut Up Knee' does NOT work. I hobbled up towards the crest of the hill, my knee throbbing with each step. It was the exact same throbbing that I felt when I injured it the first time. Was this the same injury which hadn't healed? Had I in fact caused long-term damage to my knee? I tried to stretch it out but it didn't help. I sat down, deflated.

I let out a last, pathetic 'Shut Up Knee' towards some sheep, my only companions it seemed. They looked up for about half a second and carried on eating. My mind was all over the place. All of a sudden, tears started to well up in my eyes. Maybe running just wasn't meant to be. Maybe I had injured myself too much the time before. Was this it? Was this the beginning of the end of my run, again? I so wished it wasn't as I stared blankly down at my right leg. A small tear dropped off my cheek and landed right in the middle of the 'U' in 'Up' of 'Shut up Knee'.

I have no idea how long I was there for and I don't really even remember getting up but the next thing I knew I was half walking, half hopping up the long hill towards Strathy. The next town, Bettyhill, where I'd hopefully manage to find somewhere to stay, was a good four hours away. I just needed to lie down, close my eyes and dream the pain away.

I hobbled on like an old cripple until I stumbled upon a sign saying Strathy Inn. I really didn't expect anything until Bettyhill. Finally, I thought, the Karma Gods were looking after me.

'Please be open. Please!' I begged to no one, except trusty Little Flying Cow.

I wasn't feeling hopeful as most accommodation I'd seen so far hadn't opened for the summer yet, and from the outside this inn looked no different.

I slowly walked up to the front door and took hold of the handle and pushed it down. It moved and, after a little nudge, it opened inwards taking me with it and nearly toppling me over in the process. I felt a wave of relief come over me.

'They have to have a room available. Please let them have a room.'

They did have one room left, a double, and even at £60 – which was two entire days of budget – at least I had a bed for the night.

After a long shower and a lot of stretching that didn't really seem to do anything, I lay back down on the bed and began to weep. My knee was just as painful as it had been the last time, only this time I hadn't taken a selfie to injure it. I felt the lowest I'd been in years as tears ran down my cheeks. I started to question everything. Why these challenges? Why adventure? Why running? Why spend weeks or months doing something just to get a pub story in the end? Let's be honest, I thought bleakly, that's all I was really getting, wasn't it? An expensive pub story. Was that enough? At that moment lying in a pool of my own salty tears in a quiet inn on the north coast of Scotland all I wanted to do was give up and go home.

My only hope was to speak to my coach Mark and then my trainer Steve to see if they had any bits of advice. I called Mark first.

'Hey buddy, how are you?' Mark answered the phone in his characteristically friendly manner. I felt better already hearing a familiar voice.

'It's my knee again mate. Same as before.'

'Really? Same knee?'

'Yeah. Same one. Just doesn't like running.'

Mark and I chatted for a while about my style, technique and different ways I could carry my backpack but my current setup seemed to be the best anyway. I was doing everything right so far yet I was still in crippling pain, no matter how much I was stretching.

'How's your hydration?' he finally asked.

'Really good. I've been drinking enough I think.'

'Make sure you keep on top of that.'

'Yeah, will do.'

We chatted a bit longer before he had to dash, and I was left non the wiser. If Mark didn't know a special trick then no one did. Maybe this really was the end of the run for me. I had one last hope in Steve, my trainer.

'Seano! How's it going man?'

I explained my situation to Steve.

'Have you had balls in your ass?'

'Um, excuse me?'

'Behave! Tennis balls, in your ass to loosen your glutes. Right up at the top near your hip on the side. Get a ball in there.'

I actually had a tennis ball, my second mascot, which I named Wilson in honour of Tom Hanks in the film *Castaway*, who had a football called Wilson.

'Yeah I have one.'

'Get your balls out, or ball rather, and stick it in your ass.'

'OK, hold on!'

I put Steve on loudspeaker and began to roll on the floor with Wilson right in the top of my hip and glute. I let out a loud 'Oooooh!' followed by an 'ahhhh! as Steve was shouting.

'Yes, mate, get those balls right up in your ass.'

If you were the couple in the room next to me that night, I can't apologize enough. Honestly I can't.

Within seconds, I felt my knee totally release its tension and the pain disappeared immediately, as if by some voodoo magic.

'Ahhhhh! Yes mate, that's the spot!' I shouted into the phone in ecstasy. In hindsight, my choice of words could have been different.

'Good stuff mate. Keep doing that throughout the day.

Because you don't have much running experience it will probably take you 50 days to reach some level of fitness to avoid injury but if you keep on top of the first two weeks while your body adjusts, you'll just about manage. Keep at it though.'

After our chat I continued to roll every part of my body I could think of. I didn't care if I was using that muscle or not. Forearms, elbow, moobs, chin. I didn't care. If I could roll on it, it got rolled on. I also kept thing thinking about what Steve said. Surely he can't be right. 50 days meant I'd finally be fit enough to run Britain, a week after I had run Britain.

Being sufficiently battered and bruised, I went to bed feeling a lot better than I had a few hours earlier. It's almost as if I had found a magical solution that I could call upon at any time. Wilson the tennis ball was going to be my magic injury wand. I felt like a ginger wizard. Maybe this run was going to be possible after all.

The radioactive beach I camped on

Chapter 4 – Heading South

I awoke in the middle of the night with cold sweats, which is a clear sign of dehydration. Mark had been right; I hadn't had enough water. I was currently drinking about four litres per day, but I figured I needed to make it about six in order to keep my muscles in good condition. If I did that and kept up a good dose of balls-in-ass then I should be able to manage my knee issue, hopefully. This was all speculation though, of course. I was yet to run on it.

It was a bright but chilly morning as the road out of Strathy turned into rolling hills, snaking its way through the barren fields dotted with sheep covered in their full winter fleeces. They glanced up at me briefly in case I was a lion, before realizing that although I looked like one, I was in fact just a now-clean smelling human after last night's shower, and carried on grazing.

Although the road was becoming steep, my knee seemed to be holding out. I stopped every mile or so to get Wilson out and lie on my side next to the road and, well, hump my tennis ball. Rolling the side and back of my hip area didn't look too bad. But if anyone saw me rolling on the front, . . . I'd have called the cops. Luckily, if there is a part of the UK where you can get away with lying on the ground humping a tennis ball called Wilson, it's the remote northwest part of Scotland.

After my third ball session, I was just falling into the monotonous trance of feet hitting the tarmac, snaking my way down towards the small village of Bettyhill, when I spotted a man standing on the side of the road about 20 metres ahead of me. I stopped immediately. He was on his phone and had the mother of all chainsaws in his other hand. He was in his mid-forties with years of sun damage to his face. He's had a tough life, I thought. Taking into consideration the very big chainsaw, he wasn't the kind of man you'd want to run directly towards. I got my phone out and pretended to look at my maps.

'Ya do oooh fag ooh . . . bla bla bla.'

His Scottish accent was so strong I had no idea what he was saying. He turned around and saw me. I smiled at him. He smiled back, showing all of one tooth left on his bottom jaw.

'Bla bla bla huge ginger beard bla bla bla.' He laughed out loud.

I laughed back nervously and looked around in case by some miracle there was another chap with a huge ginger beard behind me. Someone to recruit to my Viking army. There wasn't.

Then I heard a car racing down the hill. It sounded like Bonnie and Clyde's car from a few days back. This was it. They've come for me now because I refused their kind offer of a bed for the night. I turned around to see if it was their rust bucket, but it was a different car, a small hatchback with the boot lid completely open. That's so they could throw me in quickly. With my dodgy knee there was no way I was going to be able to run away. All I could think about was that my Swiss army knife was way at the bottom of my bag.

The car screeched to a halt right next to me as Angus-the-Ripper strolled towards me, still speaking what I'm now almost sure wasn't English. We made eye contact. He smiled again, it seemed sinister, and then at the last second he looked left and right, walked up to the back of the car, went bum first into the boot, shouted 'Go!' and the car sped off, his steel toe capped boots sliding on the ground as they drove down the hill and out of sight.

I stood there in eerie silence wondering if that all had, in fact, actually happened. The tyre marks confirmed it. Looking down at the ground, there seemed to be more than one set. I guess this wasn't the first time this has happened.

I took a couple of shortcuts through some bogs to get off the road, eventually arriving in Bettyhill. On entering the one-horse town, a sign caught my eye:

The Store BettyHill. Turn left at the crossroads.
Open eight days a week.

This made me smile. Not being murdered had already put me in a good mood and now I was guaranteed food.

Bettyhill was a sleepy hollow with nothing but a small convenience store next to a petrol station, that I wasn't quite sure was operational anymore, and a hotel on the corner overlooking the ocean. The hotel was still closed for the winter but, as the sign said, the store was open so I bought two bananas, a milkshake, a pie, two flapjacks, a coffee and a litre of orange juice. I then sat on a bench overlooking Torrisdale Bay in all its majestic ferocity, each crashing white wave shining bright against the dark blueish black skyline. This north coast of Scotland leg had been a tough start. The remoteness, the lack of food, the radioactive sand, Bonnie and Clyde, Angus-the-Ripper and my dodgy knee had all played their part. Worst of all, I was nowhere near my marathon a day target. Since John O'Groats I was also technically not getting anywhere closer to Cornwall, but that was all about to change. I was about to turn left and start heading south, finally making some actual headway towards Land's End.

I was pretty stuffed after lunch so I decided to have a nap for a few hours. The Bettyhill Hotel was still closed but the owner kindly let me nap on the floor while he busied himself painting the sea facing windows, which I imagine is an annual task what with the battering they get. I couldn't have been on the carpet for more than five seconds before I fell into a deep sleep.

'What! Hello? Where am I? What am I doing?' I said out loud to no one. For that split second I completely forgot where I was and thought I was still at home on the boat. Strangely that thought distressed me. Then it came back and all of a sudden I felt good again. It had been a tough few days, but I was enjoying this adventure. I sat up and slowly gathered my stuff into my rucksack. I tried to find the hotel owner to say thank you for the floor, but it was a ghost town, so I just shouted 'Thank you!' and hoped he heard.

Right. Southbound, I thought. The road out of Bettyhill was steep. After a mile I kept straight onto a single-track road as the main road turned away to the right over an old steel bridge. Within minutes I was alone again, running through small rolling hills, past a lake and along a gently winding river. It was beautiful. The road was so narrow you could barely fit one car down it, so every few hundred metres there was a passing place, signalled by either a square white sign or the same square but at 45 degrees, making it look like a diamond. I tried to work out the logic of square versus diamond, but it seemed completely random to me.

As I was trying to figure out the sign orientation conundrum, another one caught my attention ahead of me. It was about 100 meters from a little cottage and was riddled with what I could only guess to be bullet holes. On closer inspection, the direction of the holes seemed to come right from the side window of that little cottage. Maybe Angus-the-Ripper lived there? Needless to say, I picked up my pace and looked the other way as I dashed past.

A few miles down the road, the single track ended at a barn. The road continued but between me and the dirt track was a three meter high gate. I already knew there was a trail through the gate because I had done this section before. Last time the gate was open but this time it was locked so I slowly clambered over it. Scotland has access, or 'right to roam', law which states:

> You have the right to access most land and
> inland water including mountains, moorland,
> woods and forests, grassland, fields, rivers
> and lochs, coastal areas, most parks and open
> spaces, golf courses (to cross them); day and
> night, providing you do so responsibly.

Having spent the last ten years in southern England where many – not all, but a large percentage – of land owners greedily make sure no one but themselves has access to the land they own (and probably inherited), it still always makes me a little nervous clambering over some farmer's fence.

Once over the fence I decided it was time to look for a camp spot, and a mile later I found some perfectly flat ground in an old quarry. I knew I wouldn't get too many options to make a campfire but tonight seemed like the perfect spot, sheltered by a mud-bank, with just enough dry sticks and logs scattered around to create some resemblance of a fire. There aren't many places outside of Scotland where you can responsibly make a campfire in Britain, and in fact it is illegal to wild camp in England and Wales, something that would make my life extremely difficult in the latter part of this adventure. So while I still could up here in Scotland I was going to make the most of getting nostalgic, sitting around the campfire, and letting my mind wander.

I set up my tent a lot quicker this time. I was getting good at this camping lark. Next task: find wood. I started to scavenge around. There wasn't much but with my head torch on I wandered into the darkness and spent the next half hour finding just enough to make a small fire. I felt very manly as I dragged branches back to camp, (although some man points were deducted for using toilet paper as a fire starter instead of some dried fern or something). I'd also like to tell you I rubbed two sticks together and started an epic fire, but honestly, it was 2015 and I had a 99p lighter in my bag. So obviously I used that instead.

Within seconds I had a roaring fire and was feeling pretty darn smug about the whole thing. It had been a good day. I didn't get chain-sawed in half, I started my route south, I climbed over someone's huge gate without damaging myself, I didn't get shot, found a pretty amazing trail, and now I was sitting around a fire, watching the flames dance the night away. Life was good.

Of course the smug gods heard all that and about three seconds later they decided to open the heavens, completely killing my fire and soaking me in the process as I scrambled back to the safety of my coffin tent, whimpering. Annoyed and wet I tucked into my dinner: chorizo, an oatcake and a lemon. To this day I have no idea why I bought a lemon for dinner.

Damn you, you sodding camping mat. OK. I will *definitely* fix it tonight, I thought, as I started to take the tent down after a restless night's sleep. Also, I probably used a stronger word than sodding. I really didn't have a good night's sleep. Having to blow it up three times in the dark was getting tedious. I was feeling a bit moody already, so getting my fingers stuck to frost covered tent poles early in the morning really put me straight into the town centre of Grumpyville.

I hadn't been at all prepared for the overnight drop in temperature to below zero. To save weight I'd gone with a three season sleeping bag and half a camping mat. So not only did the sleeping bag fail to keep me anywhere near warm enough, my feet were on the freezing rock-hard ground all night. And now I was stuck to my tent pole.

'One, two three . . . oooosh!' I pulled my finger off the frosty surface, leaving a tiny bit of skin on the pole, while seriously questioning my life choices.

Perhaps my sudden downturn in mood was also due to the fact that today was the day where I was going to pass the spot where I fell over the last time taking that stupid selfie, in the middle of the road about a mile ahead. I decided not to have my morning pee so that I could piss all over that stupid rock like it pissed all over my dreams all those months ago. . . childish I know but I just needed to do something to it, like the Kalahari Bushmen do a rain dance, to give me luck as I continued south.

Packed up and busting for the loo I hobbled down the road towards the scene of the crime. I remembered this section so clearly now. It all came flooding back. It was a bright morning and I had slept in a barn on some hay bales in Bettyhill the night before after one too many ales. Unlike today, I was in a good mood to be finally heading south and being off road for the first time. To show said enthusiasm I decided to take a short video of myself while running along. For the life of me I can't even remember what I said. It's on YouTube somewhere but I'm too embarrassed to look and anyway it's not important. What is important is that at precisely the wrong moment, just as I was approaching a huge rock in the middle of the road I decided to look off to the left, taking my eyes off the path, like the complete selfie taking rookie I am. My right foot stepped square on top of the rock, sending my right leg sideways, which acted like a domino on my left leg, resulting in a knackered knee and even more knackered ego.

The mile to the rock of doom was the slowest I have ever run – partly because I was bursting for the loo and having to cross my legs while sheep stared at me every few hundred metres – but eventually I saw it. It was a huge . . . wait . . . um, what? It was a *tiny* little stone.

'Seriously Little Flying Cow? Is that it?'

'Yes it is, you halfwit. That's what you tripped on. The tiniest rock in the world. Pebble I'd say.'

I scoured the surrounding area for another rock, but this really was it. I decided it was best I just move on and sulked away slowly. It was only when I was a further 400m down the road that I realized I'd forgotten to pee in that bloody rock. I couldn't be bothered to go back so peed on some heather instead. It wasn't nearly as satisfying.

The end of my little off-road adventure involved climbing over yet another huge gate. In my mind I was now out of the domain of whatever had been fenced in, but what had actually happened was that I'd climbed into a cattle field. Thirty metres into the field and about twenty cows who were protecting their calves came charging at me. Thankfully the field was quite small and I narrowly escaped out the other side and over the cattle grid.

I was now back on a public road, with high stone walls either side – probably protecting passers-by from the killer cows. Predictably, it was now that my stomach started to rumble. I realized I hadn't been to the loo in two days. Why couldn't my body remember this when I was near, or in a pub? There was a small woodland about 500 meters ahead so I struggled towards it as fast as I could.

By the time I had reached the wood, found my toilet paper, and climbed over the small fence I had no time to go very far inland. It was too late. I just had to go, right there next to the road, and hope no one would drive past. I dropped draws and in euphoric ecstasy felt all life's problem leave me. Then, while I was in the peak of my performance I heard a car coming. I froze; life went into super slow motion. The car was getting closer, a dark blue family wagon. I could see dad driving and in the passenger seat closest to me was mum. Behind them where two, maybe three kids on their iPads or something. I thought maybe they wouldn't see me, squatting at the edge of the wood. Then, just as they passed me, about ten metres away, mum slowly turned her head. Her jaw dropped as we made eye contact. As our eyes locked, all I could think was: try and look apologetic, Sean. I don't even want to imagine what expression I actually had on my face. Hopefully not euphoria – I wouldn't fare well in jail.

It was at least two miles before I got over the embarrassment of someone seeing me take a euphoric dump. I was back onto a slightly busier road and making good progress south again.

The landscape was still rugged and wild and largely uninhabited. But I started seeing plaques along the roadside explaining that actually, people had lived here for centuries, up until the early 1800s when the community was suddenly and forcibly evicted from their homes. This was part of a phenomenon known as the highland clearances, whereby wealthy landowners in Scotland (many of them English, who didn't even live on the land) forced their tenants to move out of their villages and farms to make way for sheep farming, which was more profitable. In Strathnaver, the valley I was running along, if people tried to resist, their homes were set on fire. I'd read about the highland clearances before, but seeing these sad piles of stones, overgrown and dotted around the fields, and knowing that it had once been a thriving village, really brought home how unfair it was, and how sad.

As I plodded down the road I felt a bit depressed about the human race and how greedy we can all be for our own progress. I was really becoming angry and didn't like where my mind was going. Running through Britain was meant to inspire me, not depress me. I figured I was feeling down probably because I was overtired so decided it was time for a nap. Without thought or care I walked no more than two metres off the side of the road, used my backpack as a pillow and was fast asleep within seconds.

About half an hour later: 'Sir, Sir, are you all right?' A man was standing over me.

I sat up in a daze and what seemed to be an unhealthy amount of drool came trickling out my beard.

'Um, yes thanks, I'm good thanks. How are you?'

I've no idea why I asked him how he was. He was clearly distressed.

'Jeez pal. Thought yous were dead.' His Scottish accent was strangely soothing. When I do eventually die I'd quite like this chap to be the bearer of the bad news – or good news if you don't particularly like me. The man, in his early twenties, looked like he'd seen a ghost. I was still in dreamland trying to wipe away my drool.

'It's OK mate. I was just having a nap.'

'Oh. OK. Maybe next time do it somewhere hidden. You scared the life out of me. It looked like you'd been run over or something.'

'I'm so sorry,' I replied trying to look and sound more sincere than my demeanour probably suggested; all sleepy and drooling.

We chatted for a little longer before another car came the other way and he had to move his van, which he'd stopped in the middle of the road in a frantic hurry to rescue me. His parting gift was a banana. I ate it immediately.

The undulating single-track road, followed the River Naver, which seemed to be a very popular fishing river, or beat as they are called. Suddenly all these fisherman (yes, all men. I didn't see one woman) were speeding past me with an aggressive urgency in their fancy 4x4s, which I'm betting hadn't left Chelsea once until now: 'There's a puddle Rupert. Drive through it to finally get your wheels dirty. Rah! Rah!' They seemed to cut every corner bombing along way above the speed limit, sending me into the bushes every time to hide for cover. They'd then reach their beat, having saved all of five minutes by speeding, only to then calmly sit next to the river by themselves for hours not catching anything. It didn't make sense at all.

I've never understood the idea of spending thousands, and I do mean thousands, to sit on the side of the river to catch no fish. The most famous fishing beat, probably in the world, is called Junction Pool on the River Tweed and it reportedly charges £30,000 a week for five rods in the water. My friend Alastair Humphreys cycled around the world for four-and-a-half years on £7,000. Just saying!

Don't get me wrong. I do actually love fishing, mainly when it's free, or thereabouts, in the proper wild and when you've caught something big enough to eat (always return the smaller ones to the water) you stop. I caught my first fish in the Zambezi river at the age of five. It was a tiger fish and it was bigger than me. My memory is somewhat hazy, because I was five, but I'm told it made an amazing fish stew that night, albeit a bit boney.

The winding roads and 4x4 dodging carried on all the way until I reached the picturesque Loch Naver. It stretched far off into the distance, flanked on one side and the far end by snow covered mountains. I just stood there taking it all in for a few minutes, although it may have been an hour. The concept of time had become rather irrelevant and the only thing keeping me to any sort of schedule was the availability of food from shops, which do sadly close at some time. If it wasn't for need to know when they'd be open, I'd certainly have thrown my watch away.

'All right pal,' a young chap said from his car window. He had stopped right next to me. How long had he been there? I was in a proper daydream. I wiped my beard in case I had drooled again. I hadn't.

'Good thanks,' I said, now firmly back on planet earth.

'How long you been running, with that beard and all?'

'Only a few days, started a John O'Groats.'

'Oh!'

He seemed disappointed with my answer, possibly hoping I'd say something like: 'I've like been running for, like, years man. It's totally rad dude.'

'My name's Sean by the way,' I said, trying to change the subject and went to shake his hand. As soon as I got near the window a little hairy dog jumped up and snarled at me.

'Down boy, he's no harm.'

'Nearly no arm if he'd got hold of me,' I said, immediately pleased with my quick-witted reply. He wasn't impressed.

'I'm Andrew, Andrew Murray,' he replied as we eventually shook hands.

'Really? Any relation?'

'No, I fokin' hate tennis,' he said, smiling. I bet he'd made that joke a few times before. I wonder what it's like having a famous person's name. I almost have one. If you say Sean Conway really quickly, with a slight lisp, it sounds like Sean Connery. Sometimes, if I have to call some office, the receptionist will ask politely: 'Who should I say is calling?' Followed by: 'What, no way! Is it really you?'

Idiots. I sound nothing like him and why on earth would Sean Connery be phoning PPI claims direct anyway.

'Here are a couple bananas for you pal.'

Great. More bananas, I thought.

Andrew then passed me two gigantic bananas. The biggest I had ever seen, wonderfully deliciously overripe – the way I like them. 'Until its brown, put it down,' I was told as a child.

I immediately regretted my first reaction to being offered bananas for the second time today.

'Thanks mate. These will get me through to dinner hopefully.'

'Where you heading?'

'Altnaharra.'

'Oh. Still fokin' miles pal. You best get going.'

'Thanks for the bananas mate. I'll definitely make it by nightfall.'

'Good luck,' he said and sped off, his dog still yapping away on the passenger seat.

Doing any sort of challenge, especially in the UK really does restore your faith in humanity. 99% of the people in this world are happy, just wanting to live in peace and help each other. Unfortunately we only really hear about the 1% who are miscreants. That is really, really sad.

I genuinely have no idea how I would have survived the day without those three bananas I was given. About five miles before Altnaharra I completely bonked (the term for running out of energy – not some new form of running dogging), resulting in my already slow jog turning to more of a forwards moon walk – the Michael Jackson one, not Neil Armstrong's, that is. It took nearly two hours to do those last few miles before reaching the comfort of the Altnaharra Hotel where I promptly ordered a lasagne, a burger and ale.

'You look like you've come far, mister,' said the young bar lady.

Mister? What? Am I old enough now to be called 'mister' by people in their early twenties? I guess the beard, now sporting a few days' worth of muck and leftover crisps, didn't help things.

'No, just a hike in the mountains,' I replied not wanting to reveal the truth in case I was bombarded with questions. Sometimes a smelly runner just likes to eat in peace.

'Oh right. Snow is coming tonight apparently. Heaps of it.'

Great, just what I needed, another cold night. Must remember to fix my camping mat. I'll do it when I set up my tent later, I thought.

'Is there anywhere to camp near here?' I asked.

'I guess you could camp just up the road, but honestly you best stay in our hostel out back. £30 for the night, shared bathroom but you get your own room.'

The concept of another bed after my grumpy day certainly was appealing, but I spent my entire budget on accommodation in Strathy. Another bed in a week was just too much of a luxury.

'Does it include breakfast?' I asked, in the hope she'd say no.

'Aye, it does.'

Crikey! That really was a good deal, and considering the snow and all . . .

'I'll have a think about it, but I ought to be camping as that's the adventure I'm looking for.'

'Nee bother. Do yous want me to wait for the other person to arrive before I put the order in?'

'Oh no. Both meals are for me,' I said smugly.

Realizing I was probably a crazy person she just left and went through to the kitchen with my order.

Ordering two meals has become second nature over the years and I've even come up with great combinations. A chilli con carne, followed by a Greek salad is a winner when you're not too calorie deficient and can afford to fill your stomach with healthy food. Always have the salad second. Another great one is fish and chips followed by lasagne. Perfect for taste and calories. The all-time favourite though, when you really need the calories, is a Chicken Korma, followed by a spaghetti Bolognese. If the servings are good you can expect 1,500 to 2,000 calories in total. Enough to help you get up all the hills.

As I awaited my two meals, hoping the burger would come first followed by the lasagne which would stay warmer for longer, I pondered my options. I didn't want this adventure to be a credit card one where I stay in hotels each night. I wanted to have a good old Great British adventure; wild camping, being one with nature and exploring what this amazing island has to offer. Tonight I was going to camp in the middle of Scotland and even if I got snowed on it'd make for a great pub story. My dinner came and I excitedly gobbled it down ready for an epic night in the wild.

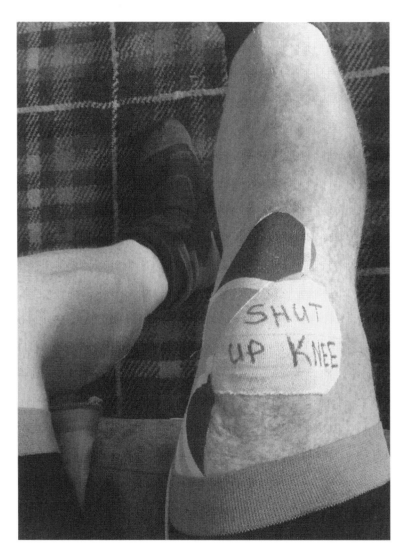

Writing SHUT UP KNEE on your knee, doesn't work

Chapter 5 – Civilisation

I woke up freezing cold, snow piled up on my little coffin tent, giving scant protection from the swirling blizzard . . . No I didn't! I woke up a little hot and sweaty from the heat blasting out of the radiator at the end of my bed. I didn't camp wild in the end. The warmth of the fire in the hotel combined with a full belly and a few too many ales resulted in some pretty poor judgment on my part, so, £30 worse off, I tucked myself into that beautifully warm hostel bed. Although the good night sleep prepared me for the day ahead I still felt guilty for staying in two hotels in the same week. I'd have to rectify that by trying to find the weirdest place to sleep that night.

Breakfast included two bowls of muesli and a fry up before I headed up the long hill out of Altnaharra. Another plus side was my knee felt a million times better – annoyingly probably down to a proper breakfast and good night's rest. What a conundrum.

The road snaked up to 270 meters above sea level before rolling down the other side towards the famous Crask Inn. I say famous with no real authority other than three people tweeted me asking me if I was going via the Crask and if so I MUST stop in for a wee dram – that's a glass of whisky to my non-Scottish friends. When I asked why I MUST stop by, they all gave a similar answer which went along the lines of; 'Well, it's just a wee nice little place in the middle of nowhere that makes you feel good.' I kind of liked that though. What more do you want from a place than to feel good.

I didn't know how far away the Crask was so just kept plodding along as the road made its way with a gentle gradient up the valley running parallel the river Vagastie. To my left were the snow topped mountains with a few brave eagles, or hawks, circling around, battling the wind. At that moment I could have been in Alaska, or Canada, or somewhere equally remote. I loved it.

An hour later, I found the Crask Inn. Sitting right next to the road in the middle of a wide open plain was the typically quaint British pub, with white walls and grey slate roof. I opened the old creaky door and was greeted in the way I like to be greeted in any quaint ye olde pub – jumped on by a wet muddy sheep dog.

'Down boy, come now, stop harassing the walkers.'

A wonderfully regal old man, dressed in a tweed jacket, looked mortified by his unruly hound. He had a gentle face and a presence that made you feel instantly at home. He was calmly going about his business, putting glasses on the shelves as if each glass had its perfect place. He seemed to take pride in it, it wasn't a chore. I liked the Crask already.

'Don't worry, I probably just made the dog dirtier. I haven't showered in a while.' I replied as we danced, toe to paw, through the door with the dog still on its hind legs, front legs around my waist. It was weirdly graceful.

After my little doggy waltz, I sat down and felt a wee-bit guilty that my shower comment had been a small white lie. I had in fact had the most glorious shower in Altnaharra, but I figured I was allowed some creative freedom here for the purposes of comedy and not to make the old chap feel bad.

'What can I get for you? Can I suggest the soup?'

Now, if any of you have a huge beard you'll know the difficulties with eating soup. Either the bottom of it gets dunked in the soup when you bend over the bowl or bits of the soup spill off the side of the spoon giving you two long streaks trailing down your beard from the corner of your mouth. It can be fairly disgusting. I've had small children on adjacent tables nearly throw up as they shamelessly shout: 'Urgh, that's gross!' as their mother, looking very embarrassed, tries to say 'Shhhhhh!' hoping I didn't notice.

'Yes, please. I'd love nothing more than a bowl of soup,' I said, not wanting to make a fuss. Soup wasn't exactly the best meal for energy but I got the impression his suggestion meant that soup was all he could muster at this time of day. He seemed to me manning the pub alone. I desperately hoped that it was tomato soup as it blends in much better with my ginger beard, and is almost unnoticeable from two or more meters away.

'Wonderful. Come through to the next room. The fire is warmer and there's music.'

As I followed the landlord and his dog through to the next room I heard the most wonderful piano music and wondered why he didn't put speakers in the front room of the pub and light that fire too. My questions were soon answered as I discovered not a radio playing the music but another man, sat at an actual piano in a room no bigger than ten square metres.

'Afternoon,' I whispered not wanting to ruin the moment. The man just smiled and nodded as he carried on playing, not missing a single note. I sat down on an old chair, my knees grateful for the rest.

I wasn't quite sure if this room was in fact part of the pub at all. In fact, after some serious eye snooping around, I eventually came to the conclusion that this may be the landlord's living room. I'm not sure who the man playing the piano was and he didn't stop once for me to ask. I liked the idea that he was just a weary traveller like myself, exchanging some piano playing for a bowl of soup. I wish I had a traveller skill to trade. Maybe next time I'll learnt he harmonica, that would be easy to carry. As I sat there next to the fire, listening to the wonderful music, drinking a pot of

Earl Grey tea with a sheep dog lying across my feet, I felt strangely proud of the island I live on – Britain. No frills, no fuss, just wonderfully old, unassuming and understated with no real desire to change or shout about anything. I could have sat there all day if it hadn't been for one huge dollop of soup – mushroom, not tomato – that embedded itself deep inside my beard, waking me from my daydream. I still had a long way to run.

Leaving the warmth of the Crask was just a little bit miserable as I made my way back onto the windy open plains. It seems everyone who told me about the Crask was right. It did make me feel good, and that was enough. I needed nothing more from a quaint ye olde pub. Nothing! Life's simple pleasures.

The next town was Lairg, where I hoped to get to by nightfall. It was still a good few hours away so I decided to put some music on and get the miles under my belt. I pressed shuffle and the first song that came up was Enya's 'Sail Away'. Whoever recommended Enya for my playlist, well, thanks for that. Nothing against Enya, it's just not the upbeat music I needed to help me run a marathon a day.

So far I was pretty happy with the kit I'd brought, but I knew at some point I'd realize I'd forget something. Today was that day. My afternoon snack was a tin of corned beef, but once I opened it I realized I had no way of eating it. I had forgotten the all-important sporknife – a fork and spoon on one end and a knife down the handle, albeit fairly blunt, probably so you don't inadvertently cut your own had off. It's a weight nerd's dream of as you don't have to carry three separate utensils. Anyway, in the absence of the sporknife, I tried to to scoop some out with my finger, which failed dismally as I cut the top of my knuckles on the sharp edges. I resorted to my trusty Swiss army knife, slicing bits out. I almost felt smug but then decided to rein it in, as I reckoned the smug gods would probably cut my hand off, or stab my face or something. They seemed out to get me. I must have been an awful person in a previous life.

There aren't many moments in life where you think, I'll never forget this, and actually mean it. It's a phrase used willy-nilly here and there but truly unforgettable moments – the ones you repeat over and over again sitting in a chair in the retirement home – are very rare. For example, I remember once sitting on the top of a hill in the Himalayas on a glorious afternoon, looking down on the fields below me; Kathmandu a haze on the horizon. I was sitting there minding my own business, when something happened. I can't remember exactly what it was now, genuinely I can't. It could have been a five-legged dancing pony, or a heron carrying a baby, I don't know. I do, however, remember getting back to Sam's Bar that night and confidently announcing I'd experienced something I'll take to the grave with me as I sat round the fire, regaling the other wandering hippies with my tale, and yet, as I write this less than ten years later, it's all gone.

That afternoon, however, as I ran alone down towards Lairg I experienced something that I will definitely take to the grave (and I've written it down here too just in case).

It had been a gloomy day with dark clouds high above me, occasionally giving me a little shower. About half an hour before sunset the sun broke beneath the clouds, casting a magical orange glow to the already pretty impressive landscape. I took my phone out to take a photo and then right in front of me I saw all the fairies building a rainbow. OK, there weren't fairies, but I saw the rainbow start on one side and slowly arc over all the way back down to reach the ground again a few hundred metres away, near the pot of gold obviously. It was breathtaking. This was only the third full rainbow I'd ever seen in my entire life. I spent a few minutes memory logging the experience for future me in the retirement home when all of a sudden, a second, even larger rainbow appeared a few metres above the other one. It was even brighter and grander and it too grew to a full, complete rainbow. Now two of them stood guarding the Scottish landscape. My first ever complete, horizon to horizon, double rainbow. It was so big I had to change my phone to panoramic mode just to fit it in. Unlike many rainbows, they stayed around for ages as I stood there in amazement, until finally the sun went behind a cloud and they evaporated before my eyes. Life's simple marvels are often the ones that are the most memorable.

Lairg wasn't a particularly interesting town by any means but it did have a Spar shop on the outskirts. This is the dream situation. Yes, dream. I dreamt about food all day, and if I could get pre dinner sorted before I got properly into a town then dinner was like a happy bonus. Food, food, food – it took up most of my thought process all day, every day. I'd have cured cancer by now if I hadn't been focusing on the carb/fat/protein percentages of corned beef with an apple flavoured oatcake – an awful combination to try and eat together by the way.

Pre dinner may be been courtesy of Spar, but I'd ended up in a pretty fancy hotel for actual dinner – The Lairg Highland Hotel. Well, I say fancy because I saw a photo of the rooms and each bed had about a hundred small pillows on them – you know, the ones you just throw on the floor, and those end-of-bed frilly covers that serve no purpose.

'Good. Evening. Have. You. Walked. A. Long. Way?' Asked a lady, in her mid-forties, from the table next to me. She was talking really slowly, over-enunciating each word while doing the universal finger sign for walking – you know the one – although her fingers weren't really moving that much so she just looked like a middle-class white granny gangsta wannabe, giving me the upside down V sign. Although my friend Derek, who is a real gangsta wannabe, told me that to successfully do the upside down V sign, is all in the elbow.

'Lift your like elbow yeah – den you is well gangsta like.' He's from Fulham.

'Yeah, I'm just running from John O'Groats to Land's End.' I replied. The granny took down her gangsta fingers and sat up straight.

'Oh, you're English.'

'Kind of, I guess.' I replied. I have four passports, or have access to four at least. I only use one, my Irish one, but I have lived in England for 13 years so it's often just easier to say yes. Well, unless I'm in Ireland of course, although no one believes me and I often have to show them my passport. I'm a right plastic paddy I guess – even though in my heart I feel somewhat Irish. It's all the ginger I guess.

'Oh, I'm so sorry. We thought you were German,' she continued, while her husband hid behind the wine list.

'Don't worry. I actually get that a lot,' I replied. This is true. When I cycled around the world, German was the most common assumption by people I met. I've never thought I looked particularly German, you know, being GINGER and all. I've never met one ginger German although the internet tells me that 2-4% of Germans are ginger. That's still nowhere near Scotland, Ireland and a small region east of Moscow where the figure is over 10%, so surely you'd guess one of those. Maybe I should learn some German and roll with it. I can actually speak Afrikaans and with the right accent I guess a non-German person would believe I was speaking German. Brilliant. I've just invented a potentially fun game for future Sean.

We chatted for a while longer about how it's 'surely the wrong time of year to do a run' and the inevitable 'at least it's all downhill, pal.' They were friendly though, and it was actually nice having a proper conversation with someone other than Little Flying Cow.

'Bollocks! I've gone soft,' I said out loud as I left the comfort of that hotel. It was so cold out. I remembered seeing an old disused building near the Spar and now that it was dark figured I could sneak around the back and set up camp. It wasn't exactly the amazing wild camping spot I had dreamed of, but after an unscheduled extra night in a hotel I figured this was karma. The abandoned building was in fact an old pub, although not a particular nice one. No wonder it closed down. At least I had a patch of ground to sleep on. I was asleep in seconds.

Oh, come on! My bloody camping mat still had a hole. Well, obviously, as they don't self-heal and I hadn't fixed it. Together with the wind bashing my tent all night and some lads-lads-lads-oi-oi-types sneaking around me at bugger-off-I'm-sleeping o'clock, I hardly slept a wink. It should be called hardly slept a blink, by the way. Who falls a sleep with only one eye?

'I need to fix this now,' I said out loud, startling a few crows out of the tree above me. The combination of the cold and lack of sleep made me sound a bit like Johnny Cash. That was cool.

I foraged around in my rucksack until I found the little stuff sack with all my bits in it, including some sandpaper, a lighter, my Swiss army knife, some string and my self-stick patches, which are actually made for bicycle inner tubes. Ironically they are actually far less effective on inner tubes as they are at fixing small holes in camping mats, tents and down jackets. It took me all of about 45 seconds to find my patches and fix the hole. I couldn't believe it took me a week to do that. Friggin' lazy, that's why.

The mornings are always slow. I just seem to take forever to pack up my kit and then when I finally get on the road I feel sluggish and sore. I had no idea of the right pacing for this run but I felt the best when I was able to run around 12 minute miles. Anything faster and my backpack really knackered my legs and anything slower and I felt like I was crawling. This is actually a pretty slow pace but I felt it was a good balance between making it still physically challenging without taking away the adventure. It also meant I had more chance of completing my marathon a day without injury. The mornings however I struggled to get below 15 minute miles, my legs screaming for me to stop for at least an hour before they warmed themselves up against the cold autumn air.

I packed up my tent and headed out of town along a quiet back road, running along the River Shin, which flows from Loch Shin, just north of me, seven miles to the North Sea.

A few miles down the road, I spotted a car was waiting on the side of the road ahead of me. I immediately picked up my pace a bit to pretend I was running faster than I actually was – you know, to look cool and all that.

'I just Googled you. Wow. We just wanted to stop and shake your hand.' It was the couple who thought I was German from last night.

'Thank you very much,' was all I could think to say – not very inspiring I must admit.

Years ago, when I first started using social media, I used to find putting my entire life online for the world to see pretty strange. When I was documenting my earlier adventures, it was always a bit weird meeting people for the first time who seemed to know all about me – which of course they did, because I put it out there, but I guess I am of the slightly older generation that didn't really think about what I put online back then and the ramifications of it. I think people nowadays are far more selective on what they want other people to see, but that's a story for another book. Recently, though, I've changed my mind on the whole idea. Both my grandpa's left this world far too young, when I was a toddler, and all my grandparents had gone by the time I was in my mid-twenties. Sadly this means I don't know nearly as much about them as I would like. Every now and then mum or dad will mention some amazing story about them. Like when Granddad went on a family holiday in Zimbabwe and they had no fridge so decided to take a live goose and a sheep for food. Unfortunately the goose got eaten by a crocodile and the sheep became a family pet so they basically starved. Imagine if this was documented online now for me to discover. Old people are made of way better stuff than we are today and I wish I knew more of their pub stories.

So I now make an extra effort to put most of my life on the internet (except what I'm having for dinner – that's still boring-ass bollocks to put online; unless you're Jamie Oliver, just don't do it), so that in years to come my great-great-great-grandkids can one day try and remember the name for that ye olde website called Face . . . something, and dig out my archives to find out the truth behind the myth that I did in fact look exactly like a Leprechaun.

Although I'm more than happy with quiet back roads, if there was any opportunity for a bit of trail running I'd take it. So when I found a small forested road running parallel to the main road a few hours into that day's run, I headed in for a bit of an adventure. About 20 minutes later – with muddy feet and soaked to the bone because, well, it's Scotland and it rains a lot – I saw a little dog running towards me. It looked exactly like Andrew Murray's dog – the one who gave me the banana, not the tennis player. I had no idea if Andrew Murray tennis man has a dog or what it looked like if he did, although I later Googled it out of idle curiosity, and you won't bloody believe it but he actually has the exact same dog – two of them.

'Buster! Come back. Come on Buster,' I heard a man shouting. (The dog wasn't actually called Buster but I obviously can't bloody remember its name so going with generic dog name instead.) I looked into the woods and, bloody hell, it was Andrew Murray banana man – his now official title of course.

'Hello mate. Wow. What are the chances?'

'I know right. Yous done well to get here this quick, pal.'

'Thanks man. Yeah, I've been pushing it.'

'Where to tonight?'

Buster started to take a pee on my foot. I jumped away instinctively, although I don't honestly think it would have made any difference. In fact, it may have actually warmed my little toes up.

'I know of this bothy in the hills between Bonar Bridge and Alness. Nice ten-mile run off the main road into the middle of nowhere.' I said.

'Aye, I've heard of that one. The D of E kids use it. Well, yous best get going and I better get back to work before the boss shouts at me.'

'Cheers mate. Thanks again for the bananas last time,' I said, hoping he may have another one for me. He didn't take the bait and called Buster and disappeared into the woods. Andrew works for the Forestry Commission by the way, if that makes his hanging around in the woods with his dog on a work day seem less odd.

My next stop for lunch was going to be Bonar Bridge which I kept pronouncing the rude way instead of the correct way: Bon-ahh

Bridge. There is in fact a Boner Bridge in America. It's made of wood and was erected in 1869. True story. And while we're on the subject, if you go to Westminster Bridge in London at a certain time of day, the sun shining through the lovely innocent designs on the cement railings casts a pretty rude shape onto the pavement. I'll stop now and apologies for wasting at least five minutes of your life as you search this online.

The River Shin had now become the Kyle of Sutherland, and just over the other side of the water I could see the enormous Carbisdale Castle. It was built for the Duchess of Sutherland in 1907 (the landowning family who cleared their tenants from their land at Strathnaver a hundred years earlier), after her husband's death. Apparently, she had a big falling out with her inlaws, so she only had clock faces put on three of the four sides of the grand Baronial tower, leaving out the side that faced the Sutherland land, because she didn't want to give them the time of day. Families, eh?

The castle was run as a youth hostel for years, but sadly they couldn't afford the repairs and had to put it up for sale. Little Flying Cow and I would have enjoyed a night staying there for sure.

I eventually made it to 'Bon-ahh' in time for lunch. The bridge was pretty unimpressive, so I found a café and ordered three ham and cheese toasties. The waitress was pretty talkative and I was enjoying chatting to her about my run, until she said, 'At least it's all downhill'. I immediately lost interest so tried to do the *Sun* crossword instead. Which, needless to say, I failed at.

It was the wrong time of year to do the run

Chapter 6 – Into the Unknown, Again

'Freeeedommmmm!!!' I shouted as soon as I left the main road to head inland towards my secret bothy – that's actually not a bothy but a sheep shelter really. I hadn't been this excited or nervous in a long time. I felt like William Wallace, only shorter, I imagine. I tried to put the *Braveheart* soundtrack on Spotify for inspiration but there was no internet I so settled for repeating lines from the film and changing them slightly to suit:

'They can take my knees, but they'll never take my freedom!'

'I know you can run, but it's your wit that makes you a runner.'

'We all end up dead, it's just a question of how and when . . . Hopefully not in a bog near Bon*er* Bridge.'

The trail soon disappeared altogether and I was calf deep in sludge following a dotted line on the OS Maps app on my phone, in roughly the direction of the tiny little rectangle on the map that was hopefully the bothy.

The extra work on my legs took its toll on my knees as I waded through the moor, my quad muscles pulling hard on the top outer corner of my kneecap which, over time, causes irritation because the kneecap gets pulled off centre. In fact, as Steve said, knee pain often has nothing to do with the knee - and he was right. About an hour in I decided to whip out Wilson and gently roll my quad on the only flat rock I'd seen all afternoon. As always I felt immediately better and spent the next hour annoyed that I hadn't done it sooner, a scenario that would repeat itself many times over the next few weeks. Pain, ignore pain, pain, ignore pain, roll Wilson on leg, pain goes away, feel annoyed for ignoring pain.

I really felt like I was in the wilds of Scotland. My open track road made way for the faintest of paths that often disappeared altogether as I trudged my way into nothingness. The evening was setting in and the temperature was dropping sharply as each foot squelched into the muddy terrain. There wasn't a tree around except for a plantation a few miles off to my right. If my secret bothy had fallen down since I was last here and the wind picked up, those trees would probably be my only viable option for shelter. Although technically one of the most remote and alone places I had been so far, I didn't feel lonely at all. The sense of intrepid adventure that was about as far away from real life that I had come across in a while, keeping my mind busy and focused.

It was nearly dark when I saw the bothy about 300 meters ahead of me and thankfully it hadn't been blown over. I was right in the middle of nowhere. If there was ever a time to get my naked vampire-white bum cheeks out then this evening was probably it. Landing up near a cold river at

A: the end of a day's running, and

B: somewhere I wouldn't get arrested and

C: where I felt in the mood for micro-manhood

wouldn't happen all too many times on this run, so I thought I should probably make the most of it.

Now, this was not so I could wash myself – I did that a few days ago, I'm talking about an ice bath. When it comes to long distance endurance I always think in terms of four major factors: food, water, sleep and body management. (I've recently added mindset as the fifth one, as you can have all the others but without a good mindset your body just won't work either.) The first three are fairly obvious, but body management is about stretching, massage, keeping feet healthy and, when possible, ice baths. They help with the inflammation and some say squeeze the lactic acid out of your muscles. There is some conflicting research that suggest ice-baths don't work at all and we should be in fact heating our legs, but in my experience I find ice baths do work; and we've all seen Mo Farah get into a wheelie bin full of ice, and if it's good enough for him . . .

On one occasion I found a fisherman just about to empty his stinking fishy ice into the river and asked him to fill up one of his net barrels instead so I could get into it. It was pretty disgusting but it did the job. Although the downside was that there was a really cute girl at the pub that night who very quickly moved to a different table once I sat near her. What an idiot. First rule of flirting: don't bathe in a bucket of fish beforehand. I'll learn one day, hopefully.

A river in Scotland in March is about as cold as water can be before it becomes ice, so this was my opportunity to take an 'ice bath'.

I slowly started to undress, my now bare torso freezing cold as the evening wind slammed against it, giving me pretty impressive chicken skin as my hair rose perpendicular, failing in any way to keep me even the slightest bit warm. Completely stark bollock naked and questioning the biological purpose of arm hair, I put one foot into the stream.

'Aaaaaahhhhhh. It's. Soooo! Cooold!!' I screamed.

What if it's too cold? Could I have a heart attack or something? No one would find me for weeks and I'd be eaten by a snide ginger fox – because all foxes are snide little critters. What a way to go.

'Shut up! You are not going to have a monumental heart attack. Get in the water,' Little Flying Cow shouted at me.

I slipped and slid over the small rocks to a bit of the river that was deep enough and slowly sat down.

'Oooh oooh oooh, ahh ahh ahh!' I sounded like a monkey on heat.

In the first few seconds I felt that moment of panic, as my heart sped up and my lungs constricted, and then, only seconds later, a sense of calm, as I felt the water wash away all my knee and leg problems. Realistically, a lot of it was placebo effect and good old-fashioned numbing, but still, I felt good. All this time I was covering my pecker to try to keep him warm. I figured I'd just check he was OK. I looked down. He was blue and not dissimilar in appearance to that of a large raisin, or smallish prune. I needed to get out. A short hairy ginger chap with a tiny prune down there would never, ever, ever find a girlfriend, ever.

Feeling slightly better that I had fixed my legs, but slightly worse for my miniature prune manhood, I scrambled ashore and did star jumps until I was warm enough to do the windmill before putting my clothes and shoes on, without sock so as not to wet them, and headed off to my bothy for the night.

The best thing about bothies, for me anyway, is that the concept of them is pretty much as far from capitalism as you can get really. A bothy is a shelter of some kind – usually an old stone hut – that was originally used by people working on the land. They are left unlocked and anyone can use them. I love that in 2015 they are still around and available to everyone for free. The Bothy Code states that you must respect other users, respect the bothy and respect the environment. The Mountain Bothy Association, which looks after around 100 bothies in Scotland, northern England and Wales, has an aim, a phrase that I really love: 'to maintain simple shelters in remote country for the use and benefit of all who love wild and lonely places'. Maybe that should be on my gravestone too: 'He loved wild and lonely places'.

This little bothy had seen better days. The walls were cracked, there were no windows or a door and there was the remains of at least three dead sheep scattered all over the floor. On entering the main doorway, you either went left or right to each side of the bothy. Right was a no go as there was way too much faeces on the floor, as well as the most recently deceased of the decaying sheep, who I named Gertrude. To the left was a slightly more luxurious room with a fireplace and, once I moved some skulls and wool balls out the way, a fairly respectable sandy floor to sleep on. This was my castle for the night and I felt like a warrior. Life was good.

There were just enough bits of wood outside and on the floor to make a small fire and in no time the cracking glow was warming me up after my river escapade.

'Right, dinner time.' I opened my bag.

'What? Where's it all gone? Gertrude, did you eat my food?'

There was barely any food. All I could find was half a chorizo sausage, a banana and three chocolate bars. In my mind I had way more food in my bag so hadn't stocked up at Bonar Bridge – all that stupid penis banter must have taken my mind off the task at hand. Freud would have a field day with me.

There was barely enough food for dinner, let alone potentially five hours to get through the bog tomorrow to Alness – the next place I could buy food. This was a disaster. Then, as if it couldn't get any worse, the wind picked up and the room filled with smoke. My eyes started to water. What I hadn't noticed was the huge hole right behind the fireplace blowing all the smoke into my palace instead of up the chimney. In a grump I ate the chorizo and banana, saving the three chocolates for the morning. I got into bed thinking how amazing it would have been to cook a lamb chop, with a sprinkling of salt and pepper, on the end of a stick over the fire. Sorry Gertrude, but it's true. I could hear her turning over in her grave.

I slept surprisingly well considering my stomach was rumbling all night, my already scrawny body eating itself from the inside. In total I had 615kcal to last me about five hours, when I really needed around 1,500–2,000kcal. In these tough, boggy conditions, coupled with the fact that I was in negative energy already after my tiny dinner, I'd probably land up in or around 2,000kcal deficient by the time I reached Alness. Most people burn about 1.5 calories a minute just standing and breathing so I really needed to get a move on – every calorie counted today.

It had also rained heavily all night which made me glad I hadn't been in my tent out in the open moor. Starving to death, sore legs and exhausted would have been one element of misery too many for me to successfully deal with.

I left the bothy, said goodbye to Gertrude, turned right and started up the hill into the drizzle and mist.

There was meant to be a path, but with all the rain the it was now a torrential river. I could see a cairn on the top of the hill about half a mile away and it looked roughly in the direction I needed to go, so just beelined it through the quagmire.

It was slow going trying to hop over all the puddles and getting stuck ankle deep every few minutes. I had decided to go with knee-high waterproof socks. They came at a high cost to my weight allowance but today I was truly grateful I had. It's usually the smallest of cuts or blisters, the kind where you just think, 'Righto, it's nothing old boy, I'll soldier on', that are the little buggers that eventually get so bad you have to quit or cut your leg off. OK, maybe amputation is a slight over embellishment, but you get the idea.

Hop, hop, squelch!

Hop, hop, squelch!

I reached the cairn and treated myself to one of the chocolates and looked at the map for direction. South, head south and you'll be fine. Eventually, hopefully, I thought.

I jumped off the cairn and couldn't have gone further than 10 metres when my right food went straight into the mud, and it didn't stop at my ankle like the all times before. Life went into slow motion. I kept falling, the mud slowly coming up my leg, like an angry slug, swallowing me. It reached my calf, then my knee, and kept going. My life flashed before my eyes. How deep was this? Was it sinking death mud? It was way too thick to get out of and with nothing but bits of grass and moss around me there was nothing for me to grab hold of. Although I had a tracker it'd be hours, or days, before anyone ever came for me. After the selfie injury I spent three days in the same spot and people just thought, 'Oh, he's having a break or something. He'll be fine.' No one came to rescue me.

No matter which way I looked at it, if there was no bottom to this mud pit, I was in serious trouble. The *Braveheart* quote from yesterday came back to me: 'We all end up dead, it's just a question of how and why.'

The mud slowly started to engulf my thigh now getting higher and higher. This was surely it . . . Game over!

Then I stopped dead, my entire leg hip deep in the mud. Phew. I wasn't going any deeper, but I still needed to get out fast. I lunged my torso forward into a puddle. It was freezing and took my breath away, but adrenalin took over as I grabbed some grass. I pulled with all my strength but the grass just broke off. I tried the next tuft and the same thing happened. No matter what I tried, grass just wasn't built to pull people out of death mud.

Then I remembered something very important. Something I'd overlooked. Like most people, I have *two* legs and all this time my other leg – the cooler one in my humble opinion – had somehow managed to stay above the mud like a boss. I could maybe kind of put it behind me and do some sort of swimming type kicking movement on top of the mud. For the next few minutes I must have resembled those people in evangelical churches who fall onto the floor in a trance, kind of like beached trout, all flapping around. I looked like an idiot but by god it was working. Hallelujah!

Wriggling and squirming, I managed to work my way forward until my chest was on hard ground and I could do a kind of push up and free myself from the death mud, finally collapsing on the soft moss. It was the best moss I've ever lain on in my entire life and all I wanted to do was fall asleep. I knew that wasn't an option so opened my second chocolate and ate that instead.

Adrenalin fuelled me for the next few hours but then the real issue of having no food started to take effect. I ate my last chocolate but still felt dizzy and fatigued. I had finally got out of the bog and was in some forested area. My pace was slow and I felt like death so I decided to do a video blog. My video diaries are always the ones that mean the most when I watch them years later. Far more real than their written or verbal counterparts. I wish my grandad had done a video diary during the family holiday dilemma on whether to eat the sheep or give it a name and keep it as a pet. You can just imagine what was going through his head at the time.

Ten seconds later. . . Why was I face first in the grass? Oh god, I had fallen over again taking the video selfie. Will I ever learn? I checked my knee to see if it was OK. Thankfully it was. I really needed to get food, quickly, but I really had no energy at all now. I got up, put my phone away and hobbled along.

I took me another 2 hours before I hobbled into Alness and the promise of food. The first place I saw was a café a hundred meters up the road. It was the longest and slowest 100m of my life, my vision coming and going because I was so hungry. I felt faint.

'Full English, a coke, those three flapjacks, a coffee, an orange juice and a pint of water please sir,' I asked the elderly waiter who looked like he may own the place.

'Don't yous mean a full *Scottish* pal?' He looked annoyed that I'd asked for an English breakfast in Scotland. I think he also didn't like my overall appearance, covered in mud, smelly and generally bringing down the tone of his lovely well-kept café.

'I really don't give a toss. I'm nearly dead and they're the same bloody thing anyway,' I shouted at him.

OK, I didn't do that. I just thought it and did the very British thing of apologising and went and sat down.

My body wasn't working at all. It was like my hands weren't being controlled by my own arms. Maybe by the arms on the clock of my oven back home. They were all over the place. The waiter, still annoyed at me, brought me my coffee and put it on the table in front of me. Unfortunately, instead of picking it up, my oven clock arms thought I should just sweep the entire cup and its contents off the table and all over the floor. I was quickly becoming the worst customer this café had ever seen. He looked at me with an expression that said 'You English bastard coming in here and being all English.' It was very awkward.

The road to Dingwall was pretty uneventful in comparison. I stopped for a pint, threw it up ten minutes later and got weird looks from an old lady as I stopped to hump my tennis ball on the side of the B817.

By the time I reached Dingwall, it was dark and cold and I'd all but given up any hope of wild camping after my crazy day in the bog. I was also still covered from head to toe in mud so I settled into a hotel, after having the world's hottest curry, so that I could wash my clothes in the sink. I fell asleep thinking about how I would definitely pay the price for that Madras sometime tomorrow.

Muir of Ord! Looking at the map, my eye was drawn to the coolest-sounding town in the whole world. Scenes from *Lord of the Rings* came to mind and for the next few hours I fell deep into a make-believe world of Orcs, Wargs and Stone Giants as I ran towards my precious. Which, at that moment, was a beautifully rare rump steak – the underappreciated of all the cuts of beef in my opinion – and a single malt in Drumnadrochit, a village on the western shore of Loch Ness and my aim for the end of the day. I found some grass and wrapped it around my finger pretending it was the Ring – so idiotic!

Sadly, however, Muir of Ord was a little off course and after a quick Google search indicated that if I was dreaming of it being Middle Earth I'd probably be very disappointed, I decided to keep along the road just east and put my head down. In truth the detour was only a mile or so, but a mile is a mile and I needed to steal all the miles and shortcuts that I could. Marginal gains!
After getting out of Dingwall that morning, I'd had to follow large A roads. They often aren't as scary as you think because most of the time they are actually fairly wide and have a hard shoulder to run on. If you can handle the constant road noise, bombardment of wind and the occasional hoot by truck drivers trying to frighten

you (so childish) or yobs screaming at you as they race past in their rubbish cars (also childish) then you'll be fine.

With the power of the Ring, I ate up the miles to Beauly, a very quaint little village with no significant importance on my journey other than when I looked at the map I realized it was directly in line with Inverness. This was huge. Inverness was a massive milestone for me to get to as it signified that I had conquered the top corner of Scotland, and was only a milestone because of how Scotland is shaped. I liked dividing my run into these geographical sections on the map. The next section was the bulk of Scotland till Glasgow. Then the Borders. Then the Lake District. Then, well, I'm not sure. I hadn't quite worked out all of the sections yet. Although in theory I knew the section I had completed, I was disappointed in the reality of my progress. I looked at the map of the UK to see how well I was doing. I zoomed out on the map on my phone screen. And out and out. Inverness was way, way, way up in the north. I still had a lot of running to do.

The village of Beauly, with its ruins of a thirteenth century priory and plenty of lovely old buildings, felt full of history. So, in keeping with the mood of the village, I decided to have my lunch in a quaint little café instead of the big posh hotel over the square. There were a few couples dining but I managed to find a table near a plug socket to charge my phone. I had forgotten to charge my battery bank in the hotel in Dingwall and was running out of power fast. I was slightly worried about my phone losing power on this run. It wasn't just used for failed selfies, and using it as a mirror to trim my moustache, most significantly it was my tool for navigation using the OS Map app. Running along Loch Ness wasn't an issue for navigation. However, once I reached some more remote parts of the West Highland Way it was very important that I had a working phone for when conditions got treacherous. I really needed to get into a phone charging routine, and also buy a proper paper OS map for sections I was unfamiliar with.

I went through the usual rigmarole of getting my rucksack and wet jacket off and started looking for my chargers and cables, which are always inevitably all tangled up in my hip bag. I'm fairly sure cable leprechauns have raves in my bag, tying knots in everything. Eventually, all taken care of, I sat down and plugged my phone in. Just then the waitress came over.

'Sorry, but we don't allow that here.' She pointed at my phone.

'Sorry?' I apologized back. 'What do you mean?'

'Phones, we can't let people charge them here. Electricity is very expensive nowadays. If we let everyone do it, we'd be bankrupt.'

I could feel the anger raging inside of me as she stood there, judging me for nonchalantly bankrupting her business like the thieving capitalist I was; coming to Scotland, pillaging her electricity to charge my bloody phone.

Why was I so angry? Well I'm glad you asked. Let me explain. An iPhone6, or most other smart phones, have an 1810mAh battery and use about 10.5w of electricity to fully charge. If you charge your phone once a day you use 3.8kWh of electricity per year. Now, the price of electricity provided by Scottish Power is at the most 17p per kWh (it's actually often around 13p). But at 17p, an entire year's worth of charging would cost a bankrupting 66p. Sixty-six whopping bloody pence, PER YEAR!

I looked at the menu and saw that the full English, sorry, full *Scottish* breakfast cost £5.75. Wow, that's cheap I thought. Dammit! Anyway, I could come and charge my phone in this café every day for nearly nine years before it cost more than that annoyingly reasonably priced full Scottish breakfast that I was going to order. I was furious. I hate it when people just say stuff without bothering to get any grasp of the facts. Uninformed people really grind my turkey.

How many folks has she annoyed, I wondered, and worst of all I bet she hates telling people too. She's giving herself a whole lot of stress for absolutely nothing, taking valuable years off her life. If she had been 30 years younger I would have given her an earful but I was taught to respect my elders so instead I did the classic British thing, *again*, and apologized. I packed up my stuff, saying I really needed the charge for my maps and left as swiftly as possible. I was causing a right fuss as the café went silent. How awkward.

I huffed and puffed over the square to the posh hotel, ate a whole chicken, charged my phone and ended my Beauly adventure with the notably painful Madras toilet break I'd been dreading since Dingwall.

The A862 was stupidly busy but the map suggested I could take a smaller back road up a monster hill via a small village called Foxhole. I stuck the *Into the Wild* soundtrack on my newly-charged iPhone to help me along. 'Society' is my favourite song on this album. I'd write the lyrics down here for you, but believe it or not I'd have to pay some record label to do that, and I doubt Eddie Vedder would see a penny, so you can just listen to it for yourself. It's a great song.

'Café 2km left' the sign said. Why was it in kilometres? The traditionalist in me didn't like that. Yes, metric makes more sense and all that jazz, but being sensible is so boring. I was dying for a cup of tea – Earl Grey – but sadly I needed to turn right and a 4km detour was just too much for me to warrant the luxury of a hot beverage.

I turned off the main road and onto the famous Great Glen Way. I immediately felt a huge sense of calm. I love the Great Glen; it's one of the must-do walks everyone should have on their F**k It list. Bucket lists are a bit morbid. I prefer F**k It list, which are things you've been thinking about forever and eventually go: 'F**k it – let's do it.'

The Great Glen Way is a famous long-distance walking trail. At 73 miles long, it links the two coasts of Scotland, starting from the Atlantic Ocean at Fort William and finishing at the North Sea at Inverness. The Great Glen is a natural faultline, like a geological slash across Scotland. The scenery is absolutely stunning, and it's not actually that hard going for a long-distance hike which should make running it that little bit easier. There is also something nice about the word *Glen*. You always feel at ease when you hear it.

'I'm just going down the glen for a wee swim.' Or

'Did you see the stag running over the glen?'

You can't help but conjure up scenes of visual poetry when you do anything in a glen and surely the best of them all has to be The GREAT Glen.

The path reached the road and snaked down to Loch Ness. It was hell on my already knackered knees. Sometimes I needed to step sideways down, like an old man who was nervous of stairs, just so as not to fall flat on my face again.

An hour later I was walking along the shore of the beautiful Loch Ness, although I couldn't admire its true beauty because rain started to beat the crap out of my face, forcing me to stare down at my feet, using my cap to shield my eyes from being blinded by huge drops of water, almost marble sized it seemed. It's the most frustrating thing when it rains when you are about five minutes from the pub, as you remember back to all the little times you stopped for a stupid selfie with a cow that no one cares about.

Soaked to the bone I sat down and ordered that rump steak I'd been dreaming about, and a single malt. Sadly I couldn't afford the 18 year old cask so went for a standard one, which, in truth, tasted the same to my untrained pallet, although I'd probably have found fermented vinegar pleasant after running today's marathon. I had been on the road for just over a week and although I had just done a marathon, my average was still below 20 miles per day because of the slow first few days. I was going to have to probably do a week of 30+ miles per day at some point to get my average up again. But I didn't want to have to think about that. Today had been a great day with the Great Glen awaiting while I tucked into a perfectly rare steak and perfectly acceptable cheap single malt.

I have fond memories of the campsite in Drumnodrochit. The first time I set up camp here was in 2008 when I was on the first leg of my British triathlon, cycling the other way, from Land's End to John O'Groats. Next to me was a chap called James who was carrying the world's biggest rucksack – he was walking JOGLE. Walking! I mean, seriously. Wow. I was about three days from the end of my cycle and he had taken ten days to walk here from John O'Groats heading south. I remember at the time thinking he was superhuman and there was no way I'd ever be able to travel the length of Britain on foot. That seemed way above what I was capable of. And yet, almost exactly seven years later, here I was, setting up my tent in the same spot where he had, next to the old tractor, on my journey south on foot.

I don't have a TV on the boat so I tend to spend hours and hours watching videos of motivational speakers from around the world, one of my more unusual hobbies when I'm not making knives, ale, or Canadian canoe paddles. A number of them seem to agree that to be happy and fulfilled in life you need two key things. Well, OK, there are more and I'm really simplifying things here. But there are two things that really stick out to me.

1: We need *certainty* in our lives. If we are certain we have a good network of friends, are able to provide food and shelter for ourselves and our family, and won't be eaten by a tiger in our sleep, then that gives us a foundation of happiness, but we need more than that.

2: We need *uncertainly* in our lives too. If everything is certain, easy, unchallenging, then life gets dull, boring, purposeless. I know, I've been there. A certain element of uncertainly makes us pick up our game. Makes us want to push ourselves. Makes us aim higher. This is why I think the most important thing in life we can do is to have goals, dreams, ambitions and hobbies where there is a certain level of uncertainly. It may be completing a marathon, or holidaying in Troms instead of on a boring-ass sardine-packed beach in Spain, or learning to be awesome at the Badgermin (a Theremin but made from a stuffed badger). Whatever it is, it's important. Comfort kills ambition and if you are certain about everything in your life, there's not a TV big enough or car flashy enough to make you truly happy.

I fell asleep thinking about the next stage of my adventure, heading south-west along Loch Ness. Although extremely nervous, I couldn't wait for the uncertainty that lay ahead of me as I ventured into unknown territory.

Starting to lose weight

Chapter 7 – Certainly Uncertain

Uncertainty number one: it properly snowed all night. The Scottish type of snow, which, as we know, tries to kill you.

'Holey moley it's cold!' I shouted out loud and then retreated back into my tent in embarrassment because I probably woke up the entire campsite.

This was the morning I realized that taking the fabric off the end of my zips was a dumbass idea – all to save a tenth of a gram in weight. It was basically impossible to do up my zips with gloves on, and when I took them off, the only way to get feeling in my fingers again was to do the double windmill with both arms.

Another day on the Great Glen Way away from main roads almost made up for the fact it was freezing cold, hailing, snowing and windy. At the time I remember thinking, 'Yes! This part of the book is going to be epic,' but truthfully it wasn't all that heroic and I just kept on running – just like Forrest Gump.

The Great Glen Way follows Loch Ness along the northerly shore, snaking its way up and down the mountainside, often climbing way above the mist. I felt like I was running through the forests of Alaska again as the single-track road meandered through snow covered huge Christmas trees. The snow and muddy ground in the forest must have been miserable for all the deer because they all seemed to be on the road. I could see their despair every time they saw me coming with the expression of; 'Damnit, I'm going to have to run back into the bog again. Damn tourists.'

Although cold I just about had enough gear. I had my running shirt with a down jacket over it and a waterproof shell on top. I had waterproof gloves too but the downside was that I had to remove them to use my phone, which was a worryingly amount of times. There were loads of different side roads I could have taken and on a few occasions, I reached a dead end and had to scramble up or down back to the road I was meant to be on, and would have been on had I just taken my gloves off to look at my maps. Another good reason to have a paper map really.

The Great Glen used to be a muddy track until a few years ago when millions, well, £1million, was spent paving and adding gravel to some sections of the path, and adding arrows so stupid people don't walk off a cliff and kill themselves because there wasn't a sign that said 'Don't walk off a cliff – you will probably die'.

I was just thinking how unnecessary all the arrows were when I realized I had managed to get lost, again. Not for the last time that day, found myself scrambling down from a deer track hundreds of feet above towards the path below, going bum first on the mud to get down. Days later I realized those mud marks on my arse looked exactly like I'd shat myself. And I wondered why I wasn't making any friends.

A few hours further south I came to a small gate. 'Visitors Welcome'. 'Pottery'. 'Tearoom'. 'Open All Year', it read. I was starving and desperately hoped the tearoom was open. I had been running for a few hours and was freezing. I really needed to warm up. I entered the yard and followed the sign for the pottery, which was a small house covered in flowers and plants. There was no one around and I was just about to leave, disappointed, when an elderly chap came around the corner.

'Hello. Can I help you?'

'Yes please. I'm freezing. Are you open?'

'Yes we are. What ya fancy?'

'Just a cup of tea and cake if you have?'

'Sure, we have both. Come in, you do look freezing.'

'Thanks.'

I followed him inside the red stable-style doorway, which even I had to duck under it was so small. Inside was a tiny café, which looked kind of like it could have been the man's kitchen, and out the back were all the various items he'd potted over the years. They really were works of art.

It's wonderful to see more and more people making a living from their hobbies nowadays. It's an exciting time in the world I believe. The internet is bringing back arts and crafts as social media provides makers with an instant platform to reach millions of people all around the world for free. One of my best friends at junior school, Cameron Barnes, was the most intelligent kid in class – As for everything. If there was one kid who you'd have said would become a lawyer or investment banker or some other fancy pants profession, you'd have said Cameron Barnes for sure. After school, however, he decided to become a carpenter instead, and a bloody good one at that. Now he makes various wonderful things out of wood, from bicycle pedals to hanging tables. It's so reassuring to see him happy and fulfilled in life, way more so than if he had been earning six figures getting fat in an office somewhere. I honestly think the world is moving positively away from materialism inspired capitalism towards 'experientialism' as people favour doing cool things rather than buying stuff. James Wallman wrote a really good book about this, called *Stuffocation*.

Inspired by this book and my friend Cameron, I've recently gotten into knife making and I love it. My first knife I thought was the best knife the entire world had ever seen, until I went onto Instagram to find out what many, many people, often in their early twenties, are doing in their sheds at home. There is this one kid who makes incredibly well-crafted kitchen knives and his waiting list is months. That life option would not have been available for him even ten years ago, but thanks to modern ways of reaching people online, he can now do what he's good at, and what he loves, the ultimate goal in my opinion.

Anyway, I've ranted a lot here, but my message is this. If you are good at something, no matter what it is, there are enough people in the world who would be interested in buying your product, or hearing you talk about it, or hiring you to show them how to do it. The late British philosopher Alan Watts did a great speech entitled, 'What would you do if money was no object?' Trust me, put this book down now and go listen to that for 3 minutes and 23 seconds - you won't regret it.

I was just over a week into this 1,000 mile run now and I was slowly starting to get my confidence back in my running ability. My trainer Steve always said it'd take two weeks to find my stride. I wish I had actually listened to him. Stubborn I am!

The Caledonian Canal, which is basically the water version of The Great Glen Way that runs from Fort William to Inverness, was originally built as passage for ships to get through Scotland without having to go around the deadly Cape Wrath. But by the time the canal was completed, ship building had come a long way and therefore ships were too big for the canal, so it never really saw anywhere near the volume of traffic it should have. At least it's been given 'Scheduled Ancient Monument' status which is defined as something that is a 'nationally important' archaeological site or historic building, given protection against unauthorised change.

I continued south-west towards Fort Augustus, keeping the canal company with my bad jokes and spotting a few deer gracefully bouncing through the forest and out of sight. It was like seeing shooting stars. By the time I'd seen them out of the corner of my eye and moved my head they were gone, into the undergrowth.

Fort Augustus was my early stop for the evening and I settled in to the pub next to the locks for a hearty lasagne and a whisky with the intention of doing another five miles into the night to get nearer towards Fort William for the following evening.

'You run far pal?' A wonderfully happy chap, probably fuelled by a few whiskies, invited himself to sit next to me. He could hardly get his words out in his excitement and with his heavy Scottish accent I could barely understand him.

'Just from Drum, mate.' I replied not wanting to get bombarded with questions.

'Wow, that's fekin' far mate, you need a whisky, barman get this man a dram.' He said in one long quick sentence with no gaps.

Dammit. Maybe I'd have got a bottle if I had said John O'Groats. Oh well.

'Alistair!' He blurted out as we shook hands but didn't quite connect properly, meaning I ended up shaking his pinkie finger.

'So what are you running away from, pal?' he laughed, saving us from the awkwardness. 'Just kidding, good on ya pal I can't run. The only thing I run is a bath now and then I also work in the Highland Clan Museum. It's just down the way over the bridge, how long you here for – can I show you it? You'd love it it's proper.'

It was impossible to get a word in with his long sentences with no punctuation. He reminded me of Spud's interview from the film *Trainspotting*.

Four more whiskies and the promise of a free night's sleep had obliterated any ambition of me doing those extra five miles. Alistair and I staggered across the road and into the Highland Clan

Museum. The first room was really just a gift shop, but the room off to the right was way more interesting. Alastair had turned this into a replica clansman home. It really was well done and very authentic. I felt like William Wallace again, coming home a little worse for wear – after a long day fighting English people and not from five glasses of whisky, obviously.

In fact, William Wallace was hanged in 1305, and they reckon the first record of distilling in Scotland was in 1494, so being the worse for wear from whisky probably wasn't an option for him. The earliest commercial distilleries were first taxed around the middle of the seventeenth century, and by the early eighteenth century there were hundreds of – mostly illegal – distilleries all over Scotland.

It's worth noting that around this point in history England and Scotland decided to stop fighting each other and created the Act of Union, a treaty uniting the countries into one kingdom by the name of Great Britain. So the world chilled out a little as soon as whisky becomes commercially available. Coincidence? I think not.

'Honey, go kill some English people.'

'Aye, but let me have a wee dram first.'

Five wee drams later. . .

'Aye screw it, cannae be arsed, I'll kill the morrow.'

Alistair was laying a brown piece of fabric on the floor. 'Sean come here pal, lie on the floor, put this on.'

'This is a proper Scottish kilt.'

I lay down and he began wrapping it around me.

'Right, stand up.'

I stood up and he took the end bit of fabric and wrapped it over my right shoulder.

'Ai man, you look like a fekin' warrior, pal.'

He ran over to a box and got out a massive sword and a deer skin shield and handed it to me. God, I felt empowered, even though technically I was wearing a dress.

'This is awesome, Alastair. Thanks for showing me this and letting me stay but I really need to get to sleep now.'

'Aye, nee bother but can I show you a quick film about clan history, honest won't take long.'

'Sure, mate.' I was knackered and a little tipsy but I didn't want to disrespect his hospitality.

'Great, lemmy get the screen down, won't be long.

Fifty minutes later . . .

Alastair's 'quick' film was a fully re-enacted documentary that lasted nearly an hour. As much as I loved learning about how awesome Scotland is and how awful the English were/are I could barely keep my eyes open.

'What you think pal? I made that myself.'

'Very good mate, but it's now way past my bedtime.'

'Aye no worries, yous sleep well just close the door behind you in the morning.'

I settled down between the fire and the box of swords. It had been an entertaining evening and most certainly a lot better than being in my tent a few miles up the road.

I barely slept as I dreamt of being impaled in the gut by William Wallace or by Alastair who, in his drunkenness, had forgotten I was here and mistaken me for an Englishman. (I forgot to mention he used to be a sword maker before working in a museum in Fort Augustus – you know, that classic life progression.)

Fort William was the next major town on my route and I really hoped to be there by nightfall. It was just less than 30 miles which was a bit further than I had planned but I was feeling confident, and my knees were getting stronger by the day. It was about time I clawed back some of the miles I lost at the beginning to bring my average up again, although it was proving to be much harder running in the hilly, cold conditions in the last few days.

I followed the canal out of town towards Loch Oich. There was a sign on the towpath saying the speed limit was 10mph. I sprinted for about 25 metres to try and break it but I only got to 8mph according to my watch before my knee told me to chill out, so I slowed down to a wobble again. I Googled how fast Usain Bolt runs and it turns out he does 27.78mph, so he would definitely be breaking the law if he came for a little jog up here. That made me feel like a slightly unimpressive human. I looked around hoping to find a speed camera for joggers, but I couldn't see one. I then spent the next mile in an imaginary world where there was a speed camera sending fines to people who were running too fast.

At Bridge of Oich I crossed over to the other side of the loch and wandered through the trees.

Oh god. My stomach started to rumble. And then do more than rumble.

This was not good. There is no way of telling if you have sharted until you reach a toilet, unless you want to actually put your hands down there, which, if sharting had occurred . . . well, you get the idea. Either way, it's the most unnerving feeling in the world as you keep plodding along, acutely aware of your bum cheeks rubbing together, wishing to all the gods that the moisture is just sweat. I crossed my legs and I started to cramp up, my gut in excruciating pain. After a quick hunched over search, sweat dripping onto my phone, I discovered a B&B a few miles away. I needed to make it there. It was my only hope.

Not again. It was the slowest few miles of my life as I hobbled a few metres, stopped, crossed my legs, clinched my buttocks tightly together, and prayed to Sterquilinus – the Roman god of manure – or as the internet now calls him, the God of Poop. I wondered if he made people poop, or was there to stop untimely pooping from happening? Being a god and all I guessed it depended on which side of the bed he woke up on that morning. My not-so-firm gut fate lay firmly in his hands.

Thankfully Sterquilinus acted favourably on my underpants and I eventually arrived at the B&B, which was open. It crossed my mind to just ask to use the loo and be off but I decided I should probably pay for a room to warrant the damage I was certainly about to inflict.

After a severely uncomfortable 23 minutes, I reappeared in the living room for a cup of tea and some ginger cake. Geoff was a wonderfully interesting chap. A typical 1960s hippy who once decided to hitchhike to India. I'd never have the guts (excuse the pun) to do that. Sitting in the quaint B&B on Loch Oich, we chatted about his various adventures, all the while his dog kept sniffing me and glancing back toward the toilet with a 'I know what you did in there!' look on his face.

The rest of the afternoon was spent relaxing in bed before eventually falling asleep at 6pm. My gut felt OK but a bigger issue was starting to creep in. My mindset was beginning to take a tumble as the disappointment of yet another short day brought with it a stark reality. I was way down on mileage. I had only managed 6 miles today so my daily average was now hovering just over 16 miles and I'd probably only get to Fort William tomorrow, putting me an entire day behind. I really needed to up my game both for my daily average, and for overall motivation. I really didn't want this run to become a chore and I felt I may if I continued to do short days.

The next morning, Geoff provided me with a sufficiently hippy full English breakfast (yes, it was a full English, as Geoff was from somewhere in northern England). Grateful for a hearty meal, I left Geoff and made my way towards Fort William. Today was going to be a shorter day as, despite my unscheduled rest stop, I was still planning to stay in Fort William. This was so that I could have evenly spaced days along the West Highland Way towards Glasgow. But I was now a day behind schedule, which although a self-imposed schedule, really annoyed me. It would now take me a week doing an extra few hours each day to claw back the miles I left in Geoff's toilet. Hopefully Sterquilinus would be in a good mood from now on.

Although breakfast was substantial, it only got me from being in negative energy back up to zero. I should really have had another meal to get me into positive energy, so progress was slow, but the route along the Caledonian Canal was at least flat and the sun even managed to come out a little, which always helps with motivation and speed (even though I was still nowhere near the 10mph speed limit!).

By mid-morning I was running along the north banks of Loch Lochy. What's more interesting about Loch Lochy other than its name, which is pretty unimaginative, is that it has a terrifying monster with an equally terrifying name of . . . Lizzie. Yup, Lizzie the Loch Lochy monster. Repeat that fast ten times. She apparently looks like a Plesiosaur, which for those who don't know is basically exactly like the Loch Ness monster. I know what you're thinking: damn Loch Lochy trying to steal the 'success' of the Loch Ness monster. But Lizzie's first recorded sighting was in 1929, four years before the Loch Ness monster was first reported. So who knows, maybe Lizzie and Nessie are the same monster.

Mind = blown. You're welcome.

By the end of Loch Lochy I had no energy left in my cement-filled legs. My run had turned to a drunken shuffle as I could barely lift my feet off the ground. Life was in black and white. There was a small town that I hoped would have a café, but after asking everyone I passed, it seemed I was out of luck. I'd somehow have to make Fort William, a further seven miles away, or two hours in my fatigued state, on an empty stomach. I turned off the road and onto the canal path again ready for an uncomfortable few hours. I passed a garage on the side of the loch. At first it looked empty but then I saw someone inside. Maybe they'd know somewhere closer for food.

'Morning Pal?' I said to the young chap in the back, over-emphasising a look of despair to encourage him to want to help me.

'Hey. You alright?' he replied.

'Sorry to bother mate but I've run out of food. Is there anywhere round her to get some lunch?'

'Mmm. Not really pal. Fort William is the next stop.'

'Really. Nothing closer?'

'Sorry mate. Nothing around here.'

'OK, no worries. Thanks mate.' I said and turned around, head hung low, ready to do the next few hours on an empty belly. The chap must have seen the look of despair on my face and just before I reached the door he shouted after me.

'Mate. If you're desperate there's an old tin of baked beans in the back of the cupboard here. It's been there for a while but it's probably still in date if you fancy it.'

'Really?' my face lit up and I stood tall again. 'That would be amazing mate. Thank you so much.'

We sat for half an hour as I devoured the baked beans, some bread and a cup of tea. This chap really didn't need to help me considering it was due to my lack of planning that resulted in me running out of food. It's not like I had a broken leg or anything. The kindness of strangers really is something the world needs to celebrate. One day I may start a news channel that is just dedicated to selfless acts of kindness – to counteract all the bollocks that we hear about in the normal news of late.

Life turned back into full colour HD and I pranced along singing songs from *The Sound of Music* all the way into Fort William. What a difference food makes. I got my permanent marker out and wrote on my arm 'Eat NOW!', hoping it would remind me to eat more going forwards.

'Hello *Friday*,' I said, as I approached a little old yacht, moored on the canal looking all sad and lonely, covered in tarpaulin, at the top of Neptune's staircase.

Friday, full name *Friday While*, is a 26ft SCOD – or South Coast One Design, for all you sailing boffins. She is a 1961 wooden yacht I bought on the eBay app on my phone after one too many ales one night in an east London pub when I needed a support boat for when I swam the length of Britain in 2013.

The 135-day swim completely bankrupted me, so in order to get some money back I sold *Friday* to my good friend Jez who was my first skipper on the swim. He sadly had to leave when I reached Northern Ireland because, well, I took too bloody long and he had to get back to work. He however fell in love with little *Friday* and all her faults, so he was the perfect person to take her on.

His plan was to sail her from John O'Groats where I finished the swim back to Cumbria where he grew up, but this was as far as he'd got her to date. Jez had left the keys for me a few weeks earlier so that I could spend one more night on her. Seeing her now brought back so many memories from those four and a half months at sea – mostly lying in the bow cabin after my day's swim, feeling seasick, trying to get some sleep while my face was on fire from being stung up the nostrils by three angry jellyfish after I barged, face first, into their casual afternoon's swim.

It was great to be back. Before settling in I found some food in a nearby pub and then headed back to *Friday* to for my night of gentle rocking and nostalgia.

Friday's interior was cold and wet, which always happens when you leave any boat for a lengthy period of time. I had wanted to sleep in the bow but it seemed Jez was using it mainly as a store room so I settled into the main salon bunks that ran down each side of the central walkway. It felt a lot smaller than I remembered. I honestly don't know how four of us lived in this cramped space for four and a half months. I couldn't even stand up tall without hitting my head on the roof.

The one addition that I did like was Jez had put in a small wood burning stove. Sadly, I couldn't quite justify losing an hour of sleep to make a fire but promised I would go back someday, for a weekend sail with Jez. It would be amazing to have the crew all together again one day. I promised to make that happen. Maybe on the 10-year anniversary of the swim in 2023.

Saying goodbye to *Friday* was a little emotional but somehow I had a feeling our paths would cross again later in life. As I ran down the towpath I convinced myself that once I completed running Britain I'd use the money from book sales to try and buy *Friday* back off Jez, so if you're reading this then it means you have contributed to that goal so thank you . . . unless you stole this book from your flatmate in which case I want to tell you I have a particular set of skills which makes me a nightmare for people like . . . who am I kidding? I'm going to do nothing about it. Happy reading.

It was a long hour into Fort William to stock up on breakfast and prepare for the first climb up and over to Kinlochleven. It was strange running along a busy commuter road, the A830, at rush-hour — or in Scotland a rush-eight-minutes. I quietly jogged along the pavement looking into each car as everyone travelled to the place they spend most of their waking hours on this planet in order to earn that thing called money, which ironically is used to pay for the car they need to get to the place to make all of the money and to afford the house that they spend more time asleep in than anything else. I honestly hoped that most of the people I could see in their cars really enjoyed what they do, because, well, life's too frighteningly short to do stuff you hate, isn't it?

I could feel my ranting mind wondering off into a negative, hateful, anti-capitalism, the world has gone to pot, I bet one day Donald Trump will be King of England[*], train of thought, but then I burst out laughing so hard at the idea of Mr Trump taking over from old Liz that I snorted. I decided to stop judging the commuters and began dreaming of what I'd have for breakfast instead.

I had full Scottish breakfast, although minus the black pudding because they had run out — thus actually making it full

---

[*] I wrote that bit in October 2015 — I ruddy well tempted fate didn't I? You can blame me (or thank me I guess if you're an idiot) for what eventually happened. I'll gladly go down for this. Also, trump means fart, but you all know that already.

English I presumed? I wisely decided not to correct them and I headed out of town to finally start my West Highland Way adventure.

The West Highland Way was completed as a trail for walkers in 1980, and was created by linking up old military roads and ancient drovers' roads. Hundreds of years ago, travellers would use these rough routes to make their way north from Glasgow, over the hills, before reaching Fort William. After the Great Glen Way and the selfie track, which were both almost roads, this would be the first proper long trail section of the run, a wonderful 96 miles of muddy paths and treacherous passes. I couldn't wait.

Within half an hour I was away from anything that resembled modern life. No cars, no trains, no planes in the sky, no people, no buildings or even stone walls, only the sound of my heart beating and the occasional haggis disappearing into the trees, as many Scottish people always joke to foreigners. There are thousands of people all over the world who actually believe a haggis is a living animal – I like that. The scenery was straight out of the Middle Ages, but more colourful, because, as we all know, the Middle Ages was black and white.

My pace was strong too, which gave a much needed boost to team morale. I was still a day behind schedule because of all the biological upsets, but I figured if I did three or four miles per day more than I had planned I'd claw it back within a week.

'Baby steps Little Flying Cow, baby steps. We can do this,' I said out loud, because it seemed more official if I did so.

By lunchtime I had reached Kinlochleven and bumped into the first proper hikers I'd seen all run. They were two girls in their late twenties finishing up at a table just across from mine and one of them might, I'm almost certain, have even partially smiled at me as they left the pub. I was in love. I had been sneakily listening in to their conversation and it seemed we were heading in the same direction – south, which was rare as most people start the West Highland Way in Glasgow and head north. Could this be fate?

'Play it cool, Sean. Play it cool,' said Little Flying Cow.

OK! I'll wait here a few minutes, ten at the most, and then run to catch them, I decided. I was excited to hopefully be spending the afternoon with other human beings and, who knows, maybe one would land up being future Mrs Conway, or Mrs Hemingway, or whatever her surname is. I'm not that bothered if my future wife takes my name or not.

It's amazing how fast ten minutes flies by. In fact, I had already given Mrs Conway Hemmingway a 12-minute head-start and I still needed to get the bill. I waved to the waitress. Annoyingly an old lady standing between the waitress and me thought I was waving at her and slowly waddled over.

'Oh helloooo dear! I see you're out hiking. It's windy up the mountain isn't it? Have you come far?' she came over and sat down right next to me as I was beginning to pack up.

'Just doing the West Highland Way,' I replied, trying to keep my answers short.

'That's wonderful. Have you enjoyed Kinlochleven? My family have been here for years. Did you know this wee town was the first village in the entire world to have every single house connected to electricity? It was called the Electric City, you know. Many London homes at the time still had only gas,' she continued.

Dammit, old people always have wonderful stories but why now old lady? Why did you have to tell me an awesome story now when I'm trying to catch future Mrs Conway Hemingway?

103

'Wow, that's a good fact. I'm going to remember that one,' I said as the waitress brought me the bill. I gave her £20 and told her to keep the change, as I was now a good 18 minutes behind and really needed to get going.

'Well, dear, let me tell you I have a few more interesting facts about this area. Did you know . . .'

Dear god could she talk. For the next 104 years it seemed, the old lady regaled me with the entire history of Kinlochleven: aluminium production, how the village was born and how it all shut down again after the factory closed. I couldn't get a word in sideways as I stood there, my rucksack on, with my foot halfway out the door.

A lifetime later: 'I'm so sorry, ma'am, but I really need to get going otherwise I'm going to be late.'

'For what? Late for what dear?' She asked, annoyed that I had called her over and was now rudely wanting to leave.

Now 29 minutes behind and £1.93 poorer after over tipping the waitress, I ran out the hotel and headed up past the hydro-electric pipes running down the mountain that the old lady had been talking about. I could see how each house was able to get electricity. These pipes were massive.

I always imagined I'd meet my future wife walking up a mountain, or riding my bike somewhere. Future Mrs Conway Hemingway, I guessed, was about 1.3 miles ahead of me. I worked out roughly that if she was walking three-and-a-half miles per hour I'd need to run around five miles per hour to catch her before she got to the pub at Kingshouse. If she decided to carry on past Kingshouse and I hadn't caught her, it would be game over as I had no supplies to continue past there without stopping. Normally 5mph would be an easy task, but this section was taking me up to the highest pass I'd climb to. I'd be running all the way up into the snow and then down the quite worryingly named Devil's Staircase. The race was on. My love-life depended on it.

I climbed and climbed, my heart bouncing out of my chest. Maybe I would see my future wife sitting on a rock after slightly twisting her ankle so I could be her knight in shining armour . . . um, sweaty shirt, coming to the rescue. What would I say? Statistically, my pick-up lines are about as effective as roller skates on ice, which is probably why I was 33 and still single.

I thought it best not to rely on my own wit because that clearly hasn't worked in the past, so I decided to search the vast expanses of the internet instead.

I put 'outdoor pick-up lines' into Google and clicked on the first link that came up.

You're hotter than jet boiled Chilimac.

Should we give this relationship a trail run?

Ever do it in a bivvy sack?

Is that a Leatherman in your pocket or are you just happy to see me?

Hey baby. I'm wearing merino underwear . . . with 3 per cent spandex for optimum performance.

You make my resting heart rate jump to 40 beats per minute.

Oh god, they were funny, but pretty awful. Do they really work? I presumed not. Maybe I should try Scottish pick-up lines, seeing as we're in Scotland and all.

'Scottish pick up lines' I searched, and clicked on a link.

Is your dad called Jacobs, because you're a wee cracker?

Love, your tan makes Iron-Bru look pale.

Awright hun? Wanna see my Loch Ness monster?

Did you fart? Because you just blew me away.

I'm going to be single forever!

Searching for pick-up lines not only proved useless but was also slowing me down, so I put my phone away and carried on running.

An hour in I reached the snow line and my pace dropped significantly as I squelched my way through the snow, my heels sinking deep, often into tiny crevasses between rocks. This was ankle-breaking territory, as the snow hid up all the places that could catch your foot.

Despite the conditions, I decided to pick up my pace. Faint heart never won fair maiden, etc. I immediately fell face first into the snow, my leg descending two feet into a small crevasse. I clambered out and carried on running. I had lost track of the path entirely and was now just following my nose to where I though the top of the Devil's Staircase would be. The snow was getting deeper up here, and with each footstep my heel would sink further into the snow and I'd have to use my calf muscles to raise my heel out before I was able to lift my leg to take the next step.

I was just nearing the top when I saw two figures ahead of me. I had finally caught up with them! I put my foot down and my heel sank a little further into the snow than I was expecting, my calf muscle tensed and I felt the snap. I slumped over in pain. I knew straight away I had pulled it.

I lay on the ground and swore imaginatively as I looked up to see the two figures disappear over the horizon and down the Devil's Staircase. I got up and tried to walk but pushing off with my toes resulted in excruciating pain. My lower calf muscle really was torn and it was all because I was in a rush to catch my imagined future wife and had lost the path which took me into deep snow. I sat at the edge of Devil's Staircase overlooking the Glencoe valley. The mist was coming and going with telescopic openings appearing momentarily through the clouds, giving me a glimpse of the valley below revealing how high up I was. On any other occasion I would have been marvelled by the unrelenting beauty, but today I was blind to it, instead focusing my thoughts on the reality that the run may be over for me.

Getting all the way to the bottom was going to be a struggle. The only way I could run was to turn my foot sideways, which didn't use my calf muscle. This seemed to work and I made my way up to the top of Devil's Staircase. I tried to look below to see if I could see anyone but it was too misty. My only hope was that she would stop at King's House. I crossed my fingers and toes, which hurt like hell, and hobbled down the multitude of switchbacks of the Devil's Staircase and along the main road toward my stop for the night, completely ignoring the beauty of one of my favourite mountain bothies situated off to my right - Lagangarbh Hut.

I entered the King's House pub and nervously poked my head into each room hoping to see the girls. I realized that by now I was quite a state with dirty clothes and a mad limp going on, much like that of the crazy person who follows you home from the night bus. I had to admit that even if I did see them it probably wouldn't go well. After a quick scour I couldn't find them but thought they may be out back putting their tents up.

For the rest of the night I keep my eye on the door hoping they would come in. At least it kept my mind off my torn calf muscle.

I never did see Mrs Conway Hemingway again, and I had to conclude that they hadn't stopped at Kingshouse that night. Instead I had a date with a lasagne and a single malt and slept in my tent right next to the river hoping the sound of the water wouldn't make me piss myself. My excitement for the West Highland Way had been replaced with the dread that I may have an injury that would result in me having to quit my run, again. I fell asleep feeling incredibly sad.

Dressed as an original Clansman

Chapter 8 – Duct Tape Fixes Everything

Dammit. My calf was even more painful than I expected as I hobbled out of the tent. I hadn't slept well at all. It was 12 or so miles to Inveroran where there was a hotel. If I was going to try and keep my daily average up near a marathon a day I'd certainly have to do some mileage today. A full day off was just not an option. I was already a day behind so needed to take every chance to steal miles.

Doing a marathon a day was always my goal and whenever I mentioned this, people always referred to a certain celebrity who did something similar, Eddie Izzard.

'Ah mate, that's like Eddie Izzard isn't it?'

Or, 'Didn't Eddie Izzard do something similar, and he's not even a runner?'

Eddie Izzard has done two pretty impressive runs in the past. He first completed 43 marathons in 52 days and then went on to do another run in South Africa where he ran 27 marathons in 27 days – a marathon a day.

I felt like telling them that I wasn't a runner either but sadly, because I am a kind of nomad and all, I didn't have a proper back-up career to convince them. I could have gone with 'author' I guess, but I'd only just published my first proper book and it had probably only sold five copies at this point, four of which were most likely bought by my mum.

But no matter what the terrain was like on my run, or that I was doing it self-supported, it seemed that unless I ran more than 43 marathons, or averaged more than a marathon per day, I would be a worse runner than a famous cross-dressing comedian, who is twenty years older than me. Oh well, lucky I wasn't running Britain for the glory, eh?!

I packed up my tent and decided to try and do something about my ankle. If I limited movement in my foot it hopefully wouldn't put any more strain on my calf muscle. I didn't have any bandages, but neatly wrapped around one of my water bottles was about six metres of duct tape. I always take duct tape with me and a good place to keep it on trips is around your water bottles to save space.

I put my shoes and socks on and then took 1.5 metres of tape and wrapped it around my ankle; over and around the arch of my shoe a few times. This seemed to limit my ankle movement enough for me to at least make some progress.

As I was leaving Kingshouse, I looked to my right and saw Spiderman doing some stretches.

'I'm bloody starting to see things, Little Flying Cow,' I said, and carried on hobbling across the car park. This time I didn't even feel fazed that I was hallucinating; it seemed like the least of my worries.

'Hey Sean!' I heard someone shout. I looked back and nearly fell over. It *was* Spiderman, or at least a fully-grown man dressed as Spiderman, on the West Highland Way, doing some stretches. Of course, that made sense. Where else would Spiderman do his morning stretches?

'Um, hi,' I replied, somewhat bemused, wondering if this was reality or a dream and I was in fact still fast asleep in my tent by the river, drooling into my beard, peeing myself.

'It's Ross; I've been following you on Instagram. I did wonder if I might bump into you today.'

'Nice one Ross, I totally thought I was seeing things.'

'Don't worry, I get funny looks all the time,' he laughed.

Ross was training to run the West Highland Way as fast as possible for charity. He was hoping it would take him around a day to complete. That's pretty much four marathons in one day. But he chose the wrong outfit in my opinion. Surely Superman would have been a more appropriate choice of superhero outfit? I've never seen Spiderman run once!

We carried on chatting for about 15 minutes, and all the while he kept his Spiderman mask on. It was quite surreal. I kind of liked that he didn't disclose his true identity – perhaps because he would lose his super running power. We eventually ran out of running-based superhero banter and he went off at lightning pace (told you Superman would have been better) and disappeared over the hill.*

To say I was running was quite a stretch as I half hobbled and half hopped on one leg up and over towards Inveroran. I was mentally struggling with what to do about my torn calf. Should I take two full days off to recover properly, and then have a huge task trying to claw the miles back? Or should take I Rocky Balboa's advice: 'It ain't about how hard you hit. It's about how hard you can get hit and keep moving forward.'

I decided to listen to Rocky as it worked out well for him in the film.

It was the toughest four hours of my life as I hobbled along looking at the ground, in pain and not enjoying the incredible scenery as I should have. Eventually I reached the Inveroran Hotel and collapsed on the sofa in the tiny pub out back. As I unwrapped the duct tape from my foot my calf was in more pain than before.

---

* Ross went on to run the 96-mile-long West Highland Way in an astonishing 27 hours and 57 minutes, an incredible feat of human endurance.

It seemed I had done even more damage by trying to run on it. I shouldn't have kept moving forward. Sylvester Stallone, you're an idiot!

Over the next day and a half I rested my leg, did some self-massage (behave) and ate as much as possible in order to help with recovery. After that I could delay my run no longer, so with my ankle now duct taped inside my shoe, I jogged, very slowly, down towards the Green Welly Stop.

Although now three days behind my proposed marathon a day schedule, I was feeling jolly. The sun was out and the landscape glowed with a slight hint of spring. I even managed to impersonate a Highland coo with remarkable success. It turns out my ginger locks are exactly the same colour and consistency to those of a Highland coo. My hair was just about long enough to push over my eyes. I took a selfie with a coo in the background and put in on Instagram, and spent the next hour chuckling away as I read all the comments that people added underneath. To date, that photo has been one of my most popular ever posts on social media. Maybe I should add that to my gravestone as well. Sean Conway: bad at selfies/had his own postcard though/really looked like a cow from Scotland.

Another reason I was in a fairly good mood was that today was my birthday. I was a whopping 34 years old, or *young*, if you're one of those annoyingly optimistic people. Those glass-is-half-full irrits (my name for people who are irritating) do have a point though. Just 1,000 years ago I'd probably have been on my deathbed, yet today, as I plod along the West Highland Way – with the exception of my raging calf muscle, thanks to Sylvester Stallone – I felt the fittest and healthiest I've ever been, and with any luck I was possibly only a third of the way through my time on this planet.

That thought both excited and scared me with equal measure – the idea that I will have to live what I have already lived another two times over.

There are so many things I want to do while I rent this body of mine, but, like lots of people who love to be outdoors doing adventurous things, I do sometimes think about what happens when I either can't do the things I want to do, or I do them all and lose purpose. At some point my body will no longer be able to cope with the ideas I have in my head. My goals or dreams or whatever-you-want-to-call-the-graph is heading constantly upwards, but at some point my physical ability graph will start heading downwards. Where they cross each other will be my midlife crisis part two and I'm guessing that to be when I'm around 50 or just before where my ideas become harder than my body can handle.

The problem is that we're all in a rush, aren't we? We no longer expect to wait for anything. Dating is a simple swipe left or right, thus avoiding that awkward, hands in your pockets, looking down at your feet moment, as you ask the girl if she wants to have an ice cream with you. Wanting to watch a film is now one click of button and not browsing through the shelves at Blockbuster, or the listings in the paper for cinema times.

There is even an app now that summarizes a book so that you don't have to read the whole thing. The advert shows a very attractive girl, sitting having a glass of orange juice, obviously in a café or something, while she is looking at her phone, being all 'intellectual'. I bet the photographer was like, 'Right darling, we need you to look intrigued and interested yet somewhat relaxed and gorgeous, like a constipated flamingo. Go!' Below the photo is a made-up review that says, 'Just read a book in ten minutes. Amazing!' This sort of nonsense infuriates me. I bet the app just uses Wikipedia anyway. Nonsense. All of it.

When I was in my early twenties, I really wanted to be 'successful' and achieve EVERYTHING by the time I was 30. Looking back now, it was ridiculous. Imagine achieving your life goal at the age of 30 – where do you go from there?

Anyway. My point is that sometimes we just need to chill out in life. Don't expect everything to come to you immediately. Until the age of 40, Leonardo da Vinci was doing court paintings, and look what he achieved thereafter. It's better to find what you love, spend your twenties and thirties learning your trade, working hard to set a solid foundation. Rant over.

The Green Welly Stop is a famous roadhouse in Tyndrum, at the entrance to Loch Lomond National Park, and it's a fun and tacky landmark for walkers doing the West Highland Way. It being my birthday and all I figured I should buy myself a present. You can get all kinds of things in the various shops and after exactly 17 minutes of browsing I found what I really needed in life – a blow up camping pillow. Up till now I had been putting the clothes I wasn't wearing into a stuff sack and using that as a pillow. This was great on the warm nights, but on the cold nights when I was wearing most of my clothes I'd have to put my rucksack on top of my shoes, which as you can probably imagine, makes a pretty neck-breaking (and smelly) pillow.

It's not like I didn't know blow up pillows existed, I have quite a few at home, but they were all around 100g, which was far too heavy for a weight nerd like myself. This pillow however was a completely justifiable 74g. It did cost nearly £30 though, which was a huge rip off considering the ones that are about 50g heavier are about £5.99. Go capitalism! I am acutely aware that I often pick and choose when to love or hate capitalism, by the way, though more hate than love. (Hmm, as I write this on my Macbook Pro while I buy my fourth pair of trainers from Amazon, using the free wi-fi in Starbucks, I'm going to Hell aren't I?)

Feeling nonetheless pleased with my £30 bag of air, I grabbed some food before I crossed the main road and continued south toward Crianlarich.

My calf was feeling slightly sore but not sore enough to ruin my good mood as I hobbled along, taking in the incredible scenery. Scotland really is one of the best countries in the world – when it's not trying to kill you with gale force winds, snow, midges or Braveheart of course. Oh, and there is also a group in Scotland who wants to reintroduce wolves – another thing that can kill you in Scotland. Imagine that, actual wolves roaming around Scotland. I mean, it wouldn't work at all. People would forget and get eaten as they staggered home in the dark after too many wee drams. It'd take years, decades even for people to change their way of life to live with wolves. As much as I love the idea of wolves roaming around the Highlands I think it probably wouldn't work; we've all become too soft to deal with that sort of stuff anymore.

The trail meandered through the valley following the river Fillan before heading into woodland, a welcome shelter from the face slapping wind. With each step I could feel my mojo returning.

Around 5pm, I reached the pretty village of Crianlarich, which is on the West Highland Way and in the shadow of several Munros, (Scottish mountains over 3,000 feet). The term comes from Sir Hugh Munro, a Scottish mountaineer, who drew up a list of all the mountains over this height in the 1890s, and it started a craze where people tried to climb, or 'bag' as many as they could. I wonder how many Munros I 'bagged' by mistake on this run? Not a lot I'm guessing but it's something I think I may get quite obsessed by with my old age, to the annoyance of future Mrs Conway Hemmingway no doubt.

This was to be my last stop for the day so I settled into the local pub and ordered a huge birthday steak and a double single malt. It had been a good day and I needed to celebrate. On the table next to me was a couple, in their late forties I'm guessing, both glued to their phones. I figured it was something important so didn't engage their attention although I was in the mood for some birthday company. I sat down on the table next to theirs which was near the plug socket. I was just scrolling through my maps when I hear the lady ask.

'Have you come far?'

I looked up ready to answer as I presumed she was talking to me, however she was looking at her phone. I guess she was face-timing someone or something modern like that, so I ignored her and carried on looking for a place to camp.

'Excuse me, sorry, I was asking you? Are you hiking or running?' she said, almost apologetically because she knew what she had done, momentarily looking up, but not taking her general gaze off her phone.

'Well I'm just doing the West Highland Way.' I replied still somewhat questioning whether she was in fact talking to me.

'Great. It's a lovely route.' She said back, and again, didn't even glance up at me, while tapping away at something?

'I know, and it's getting warmer too. It was cold up in Fort William.'

'So you're going south?' she said and gave me the slightest glance before continuing to do whatever important thing she was doing on her phone. I started to get annoyed. If you want to talk to me, please at least pretend to look interested? It's my birthday after all you know.

Our conversation continued for about 20 minutes and she didn't put her phone down once, she could very well have written an entire novel in the time as she frantically typed away all the while pretending to have some meaningful conversation about the benefits of spending more time outdoors. That is something I obviously champion but it seemed quite flippant coming from someone so engrossed in their phone they couldn't even look me in the eye to have a conversation. I angrily ordered another double single malt.

After being annoyed at the lady for ruining my birthday vibe, I ventured off a few hundred metres into a field with grass so comfortable it felt like a down duvet. Obviously there was no internet but the cloudless skies suggested a dry night so I didn't bother putting up my tent and slept under the stars[*]. As I fell asleep I kept thinking about the rude lady on her phone. I'm not sure why it bothered me so much but it did.

The only noise around was the wind rushing through the trees, which sounded exactly like waves crashing at the ocean's edge. It soon calmed me, and it was a far better noise than my tiny tent fluttering about and hitting me in the face.

The problem with sleeping out in the open, in a field of lovely long grass, is ticks. Feeling a little hungover the next morning after one too many birthday whiskies I had the unpleasant task of removing the ticks: one on my ribcage and one that was a little too close to the nether regions for comfort.

It was a wet and windy morning, but I was feeling stronger again. My calf was 87 per cent healed and it wasn't long before I was exploring the eastern banks of the famous Loch Lomond – a

---

[*] A cloudless sky in Scotland almost never means a dry night by the way, so don't trust me on that. I did however get lucky and it worked out, probably because the smug gods realized it was my birthday and let me off for once.

beautifully long and thin 24 miles of dark, almost black water. I loved it. The eastern shore, which was completely forested, proved rugged, untouched and tough as I scrambled up and down rocks and slippery tree roots. But it was the adventurous type of running I craved the most.

This section was the last rugged, remote part of the West Highland Way. The hum from the notoriously busy A82 road on the western shore was a constant reminder that once I reached the southern tip I'd be getting close to Glasgow. It would probably take me two days to get through all the pandemonium that cities throw at you. After nearly three weeks of isolation in Scotland, where the most I saw in a day was a few sheep and my twins – Highland coos – it felt like this was going to be a daunting task.

Although Easter had come and gone and most of the hotels, pubs and restaurants were now open, there was still that time of day when they don't serve food. It's usually between 2 and 5pm, sometimes 6pm. I had taken to calling it the 'Death Zone', because it's usually the time when I need food the most, to what feels like the point of near death. It seems I always land up at places at exactly 2.07pm, when it's too late for food. (Anything before then and you can usually give the old puppy-dog-look, with the *'I'm running the length of Britain and rushed so hard to get here on time so please, please, please can I have some of your amazing food I've heard so much about?'* story.

But by 2.07pm the chef has most certainly gone home and all I'm left with is a bag of crisps, a pickled egg (because just boiling it to death isn't enough) and a Guinness, because they say it's a meal in a glass, but also because after a pint I still felt pain in my calf but I cared much less about it.

Today was no exception when I stopped at the picturesque lochside Rowardennan Lodge after the kitchen had closed. They didn't have any pickled eggs but had a load of cake, so I ordered a pot of tea and four slices of Victoria sponge and spent half an hour stuffing my face while downing cups of tea as if they were tequila shots, my hunger overriding all sense of manners or etiquette – something I am not proud of at all. If the group of Japanese tourists at the table next to me had been under the impression that afternoon tea was a traditional, Great British, genteel activity then I ruined that notion for them pretty quickly.

Feeling high on sugar after too much cake, I continued south working my way along the shoreline, which was now sadly just a boring A road and a reminder of Glasgow ahead.

Occasionally I'd come across groups of teenagers doing what I assumed to be either their Duke of Edinburgh award, or a school hike – their matching hoodies and backpacks a clear giveaway. Apart from a few who had their OS maps out, the majority looked pretty miserable as they trudged along in completely inadequate footwear.

Scotland got the worst possible rating in the Global Study for Child Activity – an F, which actually means a *fail*. England and Wales didn't do much better either with a *D-minus*. It's a pretty sad sign of the times really. I do however have to feel some sympathy for kids in Scotland because as we have seen, Scotland does try to kill you every time you set foot out of the front door. The kids probably weren't miserable, they were terrified. Maybe they should bring wolves back to Scotland. The kids would become world class runners in no time.

I ended my day's run just short of a marathon and finally feeling quite strong on my legs for the first time in well over a week. The only annoyance was discovering that exactly a marathon away from my camp spot was the centre of Glasgow.

Literally slap bang in the middle. I would either have to do a very short day and stay on the outskirts or do an extra-long day to get out the other side. I wasn't sure how my newly recovered leg would cope with the second option, so I decided to make the call in the morning.

Duct tape around my ankle to limit movement

Chapter 9 – Cake Face

My now very fatigued mind thought it was hilarious that there was a town called Drymen, when in fact everything was soaking wet.

Luckily I'd had the world's biggest breakfast a few miles before Drymen so I could carry on south, getting ever closer to Glasgow. I decided to keep along some of the main roads to claw back some miles and immediately regretted it, as I had to constantly dive into nettles to avoid oncoming traffic. But after the tenth time my legs got stung, I experienced the strangest of feelings. The initial stinging pain was now more of a burn; so warm in fact that I no longer felt cold. I also discovered that my knees were no longer sore either, partly due to the fact my mind was focused on the nettle stings, but nevertheless it kind of felt weirdly soothing. The nettle stings no longer caused me any discomfort that morning. I had reached my stinging saturation and any more nettles didn't add more pain at all, it seemed.

Nettles were in fact brought to Britain for the exact purpose I was experiencing. The Romans used them to flog themselves to keep warm in the colder climates of the north, thinking they stimulate blood circulation. I can see why. It really does work*. I felt exactly like a Roman warrior as I ran towards Glasgow, my nervousness about hitting the big city replaced by excitement as I stampeded forward in my own battle – a battle not to just survive Glasgow, but to conquer it.

Before I knew it, I had reached the end of the West Highland Way. In typical British fashion it was nothing more than a

---

* *I take no responsibility for any pain you may cause yourself if you try this at home. I will, however, take all responsibility when you become the Roman warrior you secretly want to be. You're welcome!

rusting metal arch between Greggs bakers and Costa Coffee. Much like when I left John O'Groats, I unceremoniously ran past the equally unimpressive landmark and slapped it. A little too hard it turns out, as I hurt my wrist, waved it around frantically as if I was holding on to an invisible bat, then carried on running down the street. At this point I realized I actually fancied a pie, so I turned around, ran back past the pillar to Greggs and ordered four steak bakes, a coffee and some apple juice. I then ran back, slapped the pillar again with the other hand (slightly more gently), and continued towards Glasgow.

Although I was feeling good it was well into the evening by the time I reached Glasgow city centre. I had run my first full marathon in a while but felt I shouldn't push my luck. My clothes were also really starting to smell now too and I was well over the 'Two and a Quarter Rule'. This rule states that if people start sitting more than 2.25 metres away from me, it usually means I smell and therefore makes it a bit harder to start a conversation. I then don't make any friends and end up sitting all alone and feeling sorry for myself. Because I wanted this journey not only to be a physical challenge, but also a great British adventure, I'd promised myself that if my clothes ever broke the Two and a Quarter smelliness rule I would treat myself to a hotel room and clean them. This would hopefully allow people to sit closer to me, which would help me make friends or even, with any luck, meet future Mrs Conway Hemingway. As Alexander Supertramp (aka Christopher McCandless) famously said, 'Happiness only real when shared'.

Annoyingly though, I had to have one more lonely meal on my own in my stinky clothes, because once they were washed and drying on the radiator I would be butt naked as I had no second pair of anything, not even socks. Being dirty was just becoming a way of life now. My bar was quite low in that respect. In fact, I think if I was running 1,000 miles and not interacting with anyone, like they do in the south pole, I'd probably not bother to wash at all. The dirt you build up in 5 days is not a lot different than the dirt after 3 weeks really, providing you don't face-plant some mud while taking a selfie that is. But I was interacting with people, and I was kind of hoping, although my hopes weren't that high, that I'd meet future Mrs Conway Hemingway, so a good wash was in order.

'What's the best restaurant to mask my stinky clothes, Little Flying Cow?'

'Curry?'

'Oooh aye.'

'Stop pretending to be Scottish.'

'OK.'

With my legs stinging from nettles and my mouth stinging from curry, I checked into the cheapest hotel I could find. I soaked all my clothes in the sink with every bit of free shampoo, conditioner and shower gel I could get my hands on and lay down and had the longest bath of my life. As I lay on the soft sheets I didn't quite feel like a Roman warrior but I had still conquered Glasgow and was feeling pretty darn smug about it. Life was looking up.

The next day in Glasgow was an admin day. It was day 20 and I needed to get a few things sorted, like a new pair of trainers and my first much needed massage.

I had been using trail shoes in this first section, but looking at the map I'd be mostly on roads from Glasgow all the way to Kendal in Cumbria, other than potentially a small bit of trail in the Lake District, where I'd then pick up the Kendal to Lancaster Canal, so I decided to buy a pair of comfortable road shoes and deal with any trails as they came. I went to the nearest running store and took well over an hour to find a pair that fitted my freakishly small feet. I'm a size seven. Yes, you read that right, a seven. I've always jokingly referred to them as tiny Hobbit feet, which couldn't be more inaccurate as we all know Hobbits have very large feet compared to their body. Weirdly no-one has ever corrected me. Or maybe they just feel sorry for me. Although, from a technical, running point of view, my smaller feet are probably lighter and I therefore use less energy to lift them while running.

'One day, when I can be bothered, I'll work out how much time I gained while running the length of Britain because of my titchy feet,' I said to Little Flying Cow.

'No you won't.'

'You're probably right but the thought that I might one day excites me right now.'

'You're a strange person.'

As luck would have it there was a massage parlour right over the road from the running shop. They did insist that they were not a massage *parlour* but in fact a massage *clinic* because, well, apparently if they call it a *parlour* some people can get the wrong idea of what to expect at the end of their massage. Who knew?

Luckily, Graham (not his real name because I've obviously forgotten it) was free and spent a good hour beating the hell out of my legs. I am happy to report there wasn't an awkward moment at the end, either.

I felt like a new man as I pranced along the pavement. It felt like I had completely new legs – as if Graham had removed my old ones and put a brand new pair on. It was incredible.

'Sean, Sean. Wait! Stop! I can't believe it. I just can't believe it!'

A young lady in a white coat was running down the street after me.

'Hi there,' I replied, wondering what on earth she couldn't believe.

'I have something for you.'

'Oh really?' I was very intrigued.

'Come with me,' she said excitedly, and walked 20 metres back up the road and into a shop.

I followed closely and entered the shop, which was full of cakes. The lady was at a counter and turned around and smiled at me. She had a warm smile.

'We made you something for your birthday.'

My original plan was to get to Glasgow for my birthday, which was a Sunday. I had been so confident that I had put a tweet out saying I'd be coming through and if anyone wanted to run with me they could, because it was Sunday so people wouldn't be at work. Sadly the torn calf meant I didn't get to Glasgow in time and now everyone was back at work.

'Here you go. Happy birthday for the other day!'

She turned around and held up my birthday cake, which was, what? Holy crap. It was an exact replica of my face. I was speechless.

'Wow, wow, wow,' is all I could think to say. It really was amazing. The likeness was uncanny.

She went on to tell me that she had made the cake for my birthday and then when I got injured, which delayed me for three days, she thought she was going to have to throw it away, but then, and by pure chance, I happened to be prancing past her shop today. How crazy. I could have gone to any shoe shop or any massage clinic in Glasgow but I happened to choose the one near her cake shop. The cake really was beautiful.

'Go on, have a slice!' She said excitedly, getting a knife out.

My heart began to race. I was very appreciative that she went to all the trouble to make me a cake, but the truth is that I just didn't want to stick a knife into my face. I'm really not superstitious, but growing up in Africa, surrounded by witch doctors, has left a small mark on me and I'm almost certain that digging a 12-inch knife into a replica of one's own face is right up at the top of the 'DO NOT DO' column in the *Complete Idiot's Guide to Voodoo* user's manual. (That book actually exists by the way.)

'I'm sorry, I'd love to but I'm on a no sugar diet currently, you know, being an athlete and all.' I replied sheepishly, not wanting to explain that I was illogically worried that I'd put a curse on myself.

'Bollocks! An *athlete*?' Little Flying Cow laughed.

It was obvious I was lying. I knew it. She knew it. It was very awkward.

To redeem myself, I decided to donate the cake to a children's hospital down the road and she said she'd take it over later that day for them.

I finally got back on the road at around lunchtime and most of afternoon was spent plodding along suburbia just south of Glasgow, which didn't provide me with much entertainment other than a quick pint in an Irish pub and booking into another bed and breakfast (that annoyingly didn't serve breakfast) – as it was still too urban to camp wild. I thought about the poorly children who got to shove handfuls of my cake face into their mouths. That kind of freaked me out and made me feel good for increasing my karma points at the same time. I hope they liked it.

'Pal, dunnie stop in Larkhall. Just dunnie do it, pal. Put yer heed doon and keep runnin' on through, you hear me?' said the service station attendant as I paid for my coffee and a bag of six doughnuts. He looked quite worried for me. I tend not to listen too much to people's doom-and-gloom because I've heard it all before, and more often than not everything is usually fine. If anything, I was quite excited about this place called Larkhall. How bad could it be?

It was mid-morning before I reached the infamous little town, and although I was still convinced that everything would be OK, there was a very small part of me that was nervous. The beginning of the main street into town was much like any other small town I had run through, with some new-build housing estates and pretty, well-groomed roundabouts. A few hundred metres further there was a lovely park to my right centred around a war memorial and flanked on the south side with a fairly state of the art new children's play area. Sadly it was empty apart from an old man trying to feed a lonely pigeon from the park bench. I really couldn't see any sign as to what gave Larkhall its reputation as such a dodgy place.

I was now trying to look for reasons why Larkhall was dodgy. I supposed the lack of trees in the main high street contributed to making it feel less-than exclusive, but that was it really. I've always noticed that about places. You'll notice it from now on too. Places with big trees down the streets are more often than not in expensive upper-class neighbourhoods. Treeless suburbs are almost always more impoverished. It's a bit chicken and egg, I guess. Do richer people flock to areas with big trees, pushing up house prices and driving out the poor, or do wealthier people have money to plant and maintain large trees near where they live? Or, and probably the real reason is large trees are older and were built during a time when houses and buildings were made with wonderful care, creativity, and grandeur which I feel is missing in modern glass fronted architecture.

Other than the lack of trees and a few boarded-up shops, it seemed like many other high streets. I had pretty much lost all interest in finding out why Larkhall was dodgy; it really seemed pretty ordinary, so I focused my attention on finding somewhere to eat. Five shops down was a Subway sandwich shop, which was ideal for me. The chicken and bacon ranch melt with south-western sauce is over 1,000 calories. Strangely the Subway sign wasn't green, it was black. Had Subway gone through a rebrand I wasn't aware of? I preferred the green, truthfully.

'What's with the new logo, pal?' I asked the young chap, immediately feeling silly for awkwardly adding the Scottish 'pal' to my question.

'What new logo?'

'The black one, are you going through a rebrand?'

'No. We're Rangers, pal. We hate anything green.'

'What do you mean?'

'Well, this is a huge Rangers area. There's no way we can stand for anything green. Those Celtic bastards.' He winked at me and laughed.

As it turns out, Rangers are a blue football team, and Celtic a green one. So whenever Rangers play their green rivals, the fans decide to destroy anything green they can find, including the Subway sign. It's the most bizarre act of vandalism I've ever heard of. It's not just Subway either. The Cooperative Supermarket has taken the green out of their logo and between 2004 and 2007, 205 sets of green traffic lights were smashed. They also spray-paint the grass sometimes too, it's insane. Who does that to their own town? Talk about crapping on your own doorstep. It seems they are just not welcoming to anyone who is different to them. I hope my beard doesn't make some drunken hooligan think I'm ISIS or something. I don't say this often, but thank the Lord I'm ginger.

Across from Subway was a small barber shop.

'Maybe I should cut my beard off, Little Flying Cow,' I joked.

Next to the barber shop was a hair salon and two doors down another barber shop and four doors further another two hair salons.

Who needs so many hair salons and barber shops? I thought. If you search hair dressers in Larkhall on Google Maps there are 17 in total. Very strange.

I decided I'd best be on my way so I shoved the rest of my footlong sub down my throat and hastily ran down the street trying not to choke myself to death, which in hindsight was about 1,000 times more dangerous than being in Larkhall itself.

It was lucky I wasn't in Larkhall a few months later because someone put up a welcome sign to the village. It read:

Welcome to LARKHALL.

Except ISIS.

You twats can f**k off.

It became a lot more rural after Larkhall, which was a pleasant change even though I was on a pretty busy section – the famous Glasgow to Carlisle road. For the next few days I'd be following what was the old main road connecting England and Scotland. However, since the introduction of the M74, it had become, although still busy, much quieter than it had been, turning many of the towns along its route into sleepy hollows with the best names for towns I've ever heard: Kirkpatrick-Fleming, Lesmahagow, and, my all-time favourite town name, Ecclefechan, which, when I say it, automatically turns me into an Irish drunk.

As much as I loved the rolling fields of the Scottish Borders this main road running alongside a motorway was by no means all that exciting and I just wanted to get my head down, which I literally had to do whenever a huge truck came bombing past, spraying me from head to toe in all sorts of grease, gunk, cow pat, roadkill and whatever else the tyres could flick up off the road. I'd have to hunch over slightly, drop my head so that the peak of my cap could shield my face and take a huge breath, because who knows what diseases I may get if any water got in my mouth, ready to shoulder barge the wall of spray. I'd often give myself a countdown.

'3 . . . 2 . . . 1 . . .Mmmmm!' I'd groan, wait a few seconds then open my eyes, which often meant I'd be caught out by a second smaller truck behind the first one which I hadn't seen, sending spray all over my face, eyes and mouth. It'd be a miracle if I didn't get ill.

It seems I spoke too soon.

The best cake in the world

Chapter 10 – Nearly all Over

So I know what you're thinking: 'We're glad the run is going OK Sean, but don't you have any more poo stories?' Well, stand by because just as I was starting to get some miles down, – albeit on a pretty busy road that wasn't that much fun to run on – when runner's bowel struck again, this time I'm almost certain it was from fermenting badger intestines that had landed up in my mouth from truck spray. I went from totally fine to CODE RED! in the space of seconds. I managed to climb over a barbed wire fence but I was still in full view of the road with nowhere to go and no time to get there. I just about made it to a tree in time and threw my bag clear. Phew, that felt better. I was glad when it was all over.

I wasn't 100 meters down the road when I felt like I was going to explode again. Surely this wasn't possible? I looked at the map and found there was a service station three miles ahead. If I could just make it there I'd be safe. It was the slowest three miles of my life as I repeated the buttock clenching exercise from the few days previously before the B&B. If anyone saw me I would have looked insane.

I just about made it in time to the service station and burst open the main toilet doors with a bang as it hit the wall, giving the three people washing their hands the fright of their lives.

'By Sterquilinas, that was close,' I said out loud, and I meant it.

15 minutes later I left the cubical and a chap went in after me. I heard a mournful moan. Damn I felt sorry for him.

Hmm, maybe this was more than just your standard runner's gut issues. I still didn't feel well so I decided to rest in the services until I felt better. No more than three minutes later I realized I needed the loo again. I ran back in repeating the same door banging episode. On entering, I came face to face with the chap who'd gone into the cubicle after me. He just looked at me, with an expression that said, 'You nearly killed me'. It was very awkward.

Annoyingly, my original cubical was occupied. I would have preferred not to contaminate another one with my stinky gut juice. Oh well, I had no option.

Over the next four hours I contaminated each and every one of those cubicles, several times over. There was something really wrong with my gut. I don't often feel ill enough to see a doctor, so much so I keep getting struck off my GP's register because I don't go enough so they think I've moved, but I was seriously considering it. The problem was that there was no doctor nearby. My best option was to stay in a hotel and if things worsened then at least I'd have someone to help me, rather than being stuck in my tent. The internet told me the nearest hotel was eight miles away. This was far too far to run in my current state. It was getting dark and I didn't feel any better. I decided to break my own self power rule – the one where I said I wouldn't use any motorised transport at all - I got a lift to the hotel and passed out on the loo.

Thankfully my belly seemed to recover overnight. I got a lift back to the service station to carry on running from where I left off. It had been an eventful 24 hours and three weeks into this run I'd had more pooing issues than the last ten years of my life. I hoped my gut issues were now all behind me – excuse the pun.

I was later informed by a running doctor that I probably had a thing called leaky gut syndrome which is caused by poor diet, chronic stress, toxic overload (from foods sprayed with chemicals or that are overly processed), bacterial imbalance, or overtraining, all of which I had experienced in the first few weeks of the run, however I still think a bit of badger roadkill landed in my mouth from the truck spray.

Today was day 22, which was a very significant day in my adventure because it was my halfway point in time. I had planned to try and finish at Land's End on the May bank holiday weekend so that my mum wouldn't be working and could come and meet me at the finish. Bank holiday Monday, 4th May, was 44 days from when I started, which I thought was going to be more than enough time, considering what Eddie Izzard managed to achieve – something that was constantly at the back of my mind.

As I plodded along the day after spending many hours trapped in a service station by my malfunctioning bowels, I felt a huge weight descended over me. Getting to Land's End by the fourth seemed completely and utterly impossible. The halfway point in mileage was around the Lake District and I was at best four days away from there. Would it be possible to gain four days in the space of three weeks? My body and mind didn't think so. My running confidence was at an all-time low.

This part of the Glasgow to Carlisle road was pretty much completely back in the countryside. There was a huge hard shoulder to run on and towns loomed up on the horizon every few hours, which meant I could easily stock up on food. I tried to focus. With any luck I'd be able to do another marathon today and from there perhaps I could slowly claw back the miles.

The last time I had been on this road was back in 2012. I had just finished cycling around the world and I wanted to do a relatively new idea called the Three Peaks Cycle Challenge. It's where you climb the highest mountain in Wales, England and Scotland and cycle between them. I had originally planned to do it with a friend but he had pulled out a few weeks before, so I was intending to just do it alone with my mates Jez and Jon as support crew.

The week before I set out I was at a speed-networking event at the Royal Geographic Society. When you signed up you either had advice to give, or were looking for advice and you were given a large sticky name badge accordingly on which to write what you did or wanted to do.

Mine said 'I've cycled around the world', and I was looking for people in the crowd who had 'I want to cycle around the world' written on their label, and I'd have five minutes to give them some advice, swap emails, etc. It was a great event and the master of ceremonies was none other than adventure royalty Alastair Humphreys. He too has cycled around the world but he's a rock star and I guess people were too scared of approaching him (he's very approachable by the way) and instead cornered me for all things cycling related. It was a fun, but long night and so at the last round I decided to tap out and head to the bar for ale. As I ordered my beer, a girl came to stand next to me, apparently with the same idea. Right then the bell sounded and everyone paired up.

'Well, I guess we might as well chat?' she said.

'I guess so.'

Her name was Sophie and she was thinking about quitting her highly paid job to go off and do challenges to inspire others. I mentioned I was doing the Three Peaks Cycle and had lost my cycling buddy and she jumped at the opportunity. She had just cycled London to Paris in 24 hours, so I knew she could cope with the 150-mile cycle and climbing a mountain each day for three days.

It turned out to be an amazing long weekend as we worked our way from Snowdon to Ben Nevis. The two of us cycled while Jez and Jon supported and then all four of us would summit each mountain. We managed the whole challenge in the 60 hours we were hoping to. I think it is one of the most rewarding three day challenges you can do in the UK as it perfectly balances difficulty and enjoyment.

Those 60 hours also set up our friendship for life, and the Sophie I met in the RGS who was thinking about quitting her job is now the formidable 'Challenge Sophie', who tens of thousands of people follow online. She is very inspiring and it's been amazing to see her confidence grow. That was one of the last adventures I have done with someone else. I tend to prefer solo challenges. I'm not sure why. I guess I just enjoy the freedom that being alone provides, and weirdly you often meet more people. Someone will come and talk to you if you're alone in a pub but they probably wouldn't if there were two of you sitting together.

It was 3pm and I was at around mile 20 for the day. My stomach started to rumble. It was always at about this time of day that I needed to start to consider my options for food and sleep. I nervously looked at my maps, worrying that I may not have food for hours to come. I know what you're thinking. Sean, why didn't you plan your days better? It would have been quite easy to look at the entire route at the start of each day and take enough food accordingly. Truthfully. I'm not sure why I didn't do that. Although I had done some big miles so far, I was still relatively new to the running game and I guess most of my brain-space was still working out how to do the running bit without injuring my knee or dying of diarrhoea which left little room for well thought-out logistics. A year later I completed another 820 mile self-supported run and I was way more prepared for that one.

The best option for me to get dinner and a place to camp was to divert off the Glasgow to Carlisle road to the town of Moffat which would bring my total distance to 30 miles which was very much needed. Although helping my daily average, it was adding extra miles that didn't count towards me getting to Land's End as they were off course, and on top of that it was also up a very long hill. But I had no choice because there was nowhere else to get food so I just had to grin (with my mouth closed to avoid dead badger diarrhoea) and bear it.

It was slow going and two miles before town I bonked big time. I had nothing left in the tank. My slow jog slowed even further to a waddle. I just needed some food, lifting my feet off the ground took the very last bits of energy from me.

'At least your tiny feet are easier to lift,' laughed Little Flying Cow

'I'm going to have the biggest cow steak in the world tonight.'

That shut him up.

Just then a blue van pulled up along the pavement about ten metres ahead of me. A few seconds later a pizza box slid out the driver's window. Was I imagining it, my hungry brain seeing things? I closed my eyes and fully expected there to be nothing when I opened them.

'Mate, want some pizza? Yous look tired.' A young chap, possibly a builder, was smiling from ear to ear.

'Really? That would be amazing.' I couldn't believe my luck – just when I was bonking badly.

'I've seen you on Facebook, mate. Epic effort. I got a few spare slices. They're all yours mate. I'm on a diet anyway.'

'Mate, you've saved me. Thank you.'

'No worries. Keep running mate. You keep running.' He shouted as he sped off.

My mood was immediately better, and I picked up my pace towards Moffat.

I settled into a hotel for dinner before heading out of town to set up camp for the night. Somehow I had managed to run 29 miles and I felt good. Maybe getting to Land's End by the fourth was doable after all.

Snow. Actually blizzard-like, can't-feel-your-face, eyeballs-start-to-freeze snow decided to descend. It was ruddy April! What was happening? The morning was slow, cold and wet but I felt focused. I wanted to get to England, or as close to England as possible. Completing Scotland would be a huge boost to my morale, which was seriously lacking of late.

Argh, I realized I'd missed the turning into fekin' Ecclefechan! Ha! I chuckled to myself because I'd just found my favourite phrase of all time – fekin' Ecclefechan!

Although I was only 500m past the turning, I physically couldn't bring myself to turn back and add the unnecessary mileage. I hated the idea of going backwards and anything more than about 50m was just too far. It's idiotic I know.

Nevertheless I plodded on for a few more hours until I reached Kirkpatrick-Fleming, where I had the steak I had threatened Little Flying Cow with the day before. It turned out to be the worst steak I think I have ever had which was my comeuppance I guess. Damn you smug gods.

My target that had actually been Gretna Green, the end of Scotland, but it was getting late and I realized I would need to have breakfast in Gretna, and since nothing would be open before 8am, I decided to camp four miles before it in a forest just next to the road. I was getting into a routine of getting up at around 7am so that by the time I had packed up and hit the road things were opening and I could get food.

The ground was perfectly flat with a thin layer of leaves covering mud with the exact texture you want from mud when sliding tent pegs into the ground. To make things even better there were no brambles or nettles. It's not often I get excited about the texture of mud and the flatness of ground, but this really was the perfect camp spot for my last night in Scotland. Tomorrow my Scottish leg would come to an end and three weeks of England, where wild camping is technically illegal, would start. It was nice to end on a high note in this wonderful little woodland.

I knew it was too good to be true. My idyllic little perfect camp spot turned out to be a crow's brothel or something alike. I hardly slept a wink as flocks of the damn things cavorted in the trees above me, squawking away and flapping their wings trying to impress their playing-hard-to-get suitors. Can you eat crow I thought? I swear one even shat on my tent although I can't be completely sure that it hadn't happened on a previous night. Nevertheless I was tired and grumpy and needed some food.

I wanted my last breakfast in Scotland to be the mother of all Scottish breakfasts, with extra black pudding. The Old Toll Bar Cafe, the last Inn in Scotland, didn't disappoint.

Gretna Green was made famous in the mid-eighteenth century as Scotland's marriage laws were different to those of England, where your parents could stop you getting married if you were under 21. In Scotland, so long as the boy was 14 or over, and the girl 12, any two people could just rock up and get married here, and thousands did just that. In 1929, Scotland eventually decided that both parties had to be at least 16 years old because, well, we all know we're basically still idiots up until 16, even though we think we know everything. (I however was an exception to that rule – I did know everything at 16.)

'Maybe the future Mrs Conway Hemingway is here in the café. You could marry her now?' Little Flying Cow smirked at me.

'Don't be daft.'

Although I did have a quick scour around to see if there was anyone that would be even a potential, sadly I was the youngest person by about half a century. Maybe the girl of my dreams would turn up while I stuffed my face with black pudding and I'd leave this café a married man.

After a huge breakfast – and still very much single – I crossed the road to the start of the bridge. On the other side of the small River Sark was England. I do like the irony that two nations that historically have not liked each other very much are now separated by a river so small that if you tripped you would land up in another country.

I was sad to be leaving Scotland. I may be as English as every other colonial African in the world, but the ginger Celt in me always felt drawn to Scotland. (So much so that in a few years' time I'd eventually move to within 50 miles of the Scottish border.) It had been an eventful three weeks and almost nothing had gone to plan, but I had made it this far and felt pretty darn proud of myself. I had less than three weeks to get to Land's Ends if I was to reach my marathon a day target.

This was it. England here I come.

I crossed the bridge, shouted 'Freeeeedom!', slapped the 'Welcome to England' sign, and then thought I should probably find an English saying to shout out inappropriately instead.

'Let's go pillage Scotland, Rupert?' Little Flying Cow suggested drily.

Historically that probably was quite accurate, but I figured it best if I went with a different one. I'd hate to be the catalyst that ended the eighteenth-century Act of Union. Imagine that gravestone endnote: 'He famously instigated a new war between England and Scotland.'

Breath-taking views keeping me going

Chapter 11 – Over the Border

Damn you, golden arches. And especially these ones, just north of Carlisle. This was the third time I'd found myself starving to death outside this branch of McDonalds. Ray Kroc, the business mastermind who turned McDonalds into a global franchise, did say he was in the location property business and this 'restaurant' – if you can call it that – certainly seems strategically placed for all the people running, cycling or hitting a golf ball the length of Britain. (Yes, someone has actually hit a golf ball from Land's End to John O'Groats. His name is David Sullivan. I've always wondered how many windows he broke en route.)

I really, *really* didn't want to eat there for a third bloody time, but my gut was turning inside out and there was nothing else around, so with my anti-capitalist hat buried shamefully deep in my backpack I sulked my way inside and ordered everything on the menu – all the while hoping they have sunscreen in hell because gingers don't do well in the heat.

The weather had been getting steadily warmer over the last few weeks as spring started to awaken. It was nice to be in Northern England. I guess if you live in Carlisle, you are pretty much the most northern person you can be. I do wonder what they think of people from Manchester calling themselves Northern, which they are, but looking on the map, Manchester felt very much southern from here. Northerners are statistically way more friendly than the rest of England according to recent studies. In fact more than half of all northerners will do a random act of kindness every single day. I liked that a lot – I guess that may have also played a part in me moving north a few years after my run. A bit like in Glasgow, it then took me a few hours till late morning to work my way through the busy streets of the city of Carlisle before I was able to enjoy the quieter back roads towards Penrith. I was feeling strong and was enjoying the smaller roads, only meeting a car every 10 minutes or so, a welcomed change from the trucks that had bombed past me all day since I left Glasgow. It was looking like I may run another 30 odd miles today too which helped my morale no end. By late afternoon with a clear night ahead, with no rain, I decided to stop for a late lunch/early dinner and then carry on running into the night. Thankfully almost every little village I ran past had a pub so I stopped in Wreay for something to eat.

'Is Russian the same as English?' asked the young bar lady to the old chap at the bar who seemed to be a local, or her uncle or something. That's definitely the type of question you only ever dare asking someone you know.

'What you mean, love?' asked the man. His use of 'love' meant he was probably a local and not her uncle.

'You know. Do they speak English in Russia?'

'Well, some people do.'

'What you mean?'

'The ones who learned it in school can speak it.'

'What language do they speak in Russia?'

'Russian.'

'Really? Is Russian a language?'

'Is American a language?' she continued to which I lost interest.

I do wonder how some people manage their way through life. Trying to tune out of her nonsense, I got OS maps up on my phone and clicked on satellite view to see if there any woodland to sleep in. I was quite nervous, but somewhat excited about finding a camp spot for the night. Although life hadn't changed all that dramatically having reached England, it was now technically illegal to camp wild. Plus, the places I was going to be running through would be increasingly built up, so it would be harder to find a quiet camp spot out of the way, which would make evenings much more difficult and possibly expensive, as I may have to resort to hotels and official campsites more often.

My OS map showed a forest about four miles before Penrith, the perfect distance for me to run in the morning to reach a café, as they could generally be counted on to open by 8am. The forest turned out to be more of a woodland and wasn't that deep – 50 metres at the most – so I'd be fairly close to the road, which wasn't ideal, but it was my only real camping option for the night.

I think I may have found Britain's straightest road. There are a few back roads running parallel to the M6 that are amazingly straight. I had decided to give myself a longer than usual stop in Wreay so that I ran longer into the night because I needed to sneak off into a bush after dark to avoid detection. I felt like I was a sniper on an ambush. Running down deserted back roads at night certainly has a sinister element to it.

On approaching the forest, I found that it was bordered by a pretty rickety stone wall, the type that would almost certainly crumble should I try and climb over it. I had to find a gate. About half way down I eventually came across a small red gate that annoyingly looked in pretty good condition, which suggested this forest was used and cared for regularly and not the abandoned woodland I was hoping for. I needed to wait for the road to be clear of traffic so that no one would see me sneak into the woodland so I stopped and pretended to tie my shoelace while a few cars drove past. Then there was clear patch. I ran across the road and hopped over the gate. My heart began to race. I was in my little woodland, my first camp spot in England.

The downside with setting up camp near a road, in the dark, in a woodland where you're not really meant to be, is the need for a head torch can alert passing traffic to your presence. I found a clear spot behind a tree in between some nettles and brambles and started to set up my tent. A few cars drove past and I managed to cover up my head torch, but the third one kind of crept up on me and I was quite late in turning the light off. As the car got to directly opposite where I was, it braked hard, slowing down to a crawl. I held my breath. Maybe this forest had CCTV and the farmer saw me clambering over this gate and is now coming to find me, with his dog and a gun and an army; tanks will come next, I'm certain of it. Life went into slow motion again as my mind raced away. The car travelled painfully slowly for about 10 seconds, and just when I thought they were going to stop, the brake lights turned off and they sped up and disappeared out of sight.

'You have a wild imagination mate,' said Little Flying Cow.

'I know, I can't help it.'

It's ridiculous the scenarios my mind creates sometimes. The car was probably only slowing down to avoid running over a hedgehog. Nevertheless, I spent the next 20 minutes trying to put up the last bit of my tent in the complete darkness to avoid certain detection from the spy drones that were obviously circling above, looking for a hairy ginger guy thought to be illegally camping in a woodland north of Penrith.

It's probably a good time to talk about the wild camping rule I have been so paranoid about leading up to my English leg. It is illegal to camp wild in England and Wales. This may surprise you considering some of the rants I've been on, but I think the current system is the best for the conservation of our wonderful landscape. I really don't want to promote a free-for-all, camp anywhere idea at all. In Scotland, wild camping works because they have the space. In England and Wales, I believe that the current rule is valid, as you can imagine our woodlands and pastures could get very badly mistreated and overrun, and some people would abuse the system. However, the rule that you have to ask the landowner's permission is wholly unrealistic. I mean, I had no idea who owns this woodland. It's likely to be some out-of-towner who had a spare £10k and thought it would be cool to own a woodland in Cumbria. Although I do agree with the current rules for Wild camping in England and Wales to avoid misuse, if you are going to do it these are the rules you should adhere to:

1.	Never camp in a working farmers field. There may be pregnant sheep, sensitive livestock or killer bulls. This land is for farmers to make their living from, and we all need to be supporting local produce for the good of the world.

2.	Don't light a fire. There are some exceptions, like below the high tide mark on some beaches, but generally don't do it.

3.	Arrive late and leave early. This way most of the time no one will ever know you were even there.

4.	Don't stay more than one night. There are some places where this may be possible but generally don't hang around.

5.	Don't leave any litter. As if I need to write that down. In fact, pick up any litter you find.

6.	Limit numbers to a handful at the most. Don't go out with 20 people. This is not fair. Keep the numbers low. Ideally just two or three of you.

7.	Don't promote where you camped. It's easy to find a gem of a spot and tell all your mates, who in turn tell their mates and so on. Then before you know it, it's ruined. Let people find their own secret camping spots.

So that is how I was going to deal with the next three weeks on the road in England: being respectful of the land and landowners and trying to go unnoticed.

My eyes shot open. It was about 3am and I could see a bright torch shining directly at my tent. It was hard to tell, but it seemed no more than five metres away from me. My heart raced. Maybe they haven't seen me. Maybe if I keep quiet they will go away. I figured the man or woman with the torch was probably more scared than I was. It takes balls, and the feminine version of 'balls', to avoid being sexist, for someone to walk up to a tent not knowing who is inside. I decided not to move a muscle to see if they would go away.

Two minutes.

Five minutes.

Ten minutes. And besides the torch flickering now and then, they hadn't moved.

Say something scary and they'll run away, I thought.

I didn't know what to do. If this was the landowner then I could be reprimanded for trespassing – and rightly so. Dammit, I thought they were an out-of-towner!

OK. I'm going to say something. Right here goes.

'Go away. Leave me alone!' I shouted with all the gusto and bravery of the Roman warrior I wanted to be.

The light didn't move. It just stayed on, pointing at me only metres away.

Maybe I should put my head out the flap. Surely my very hairy dirty face would deter anyone from hassling me – the perks of an unwashed beard. I slowly unzipped my tent and put on the most bad-ass face I could, ready to confront my torch-wielding nemesis in the darkness.

'GO AWAY!' I howled, and let out an almighty roar that wouldn't be amiss on the African plains. I then looked right into the face of my enemy and . . . wait, what? There was no one there. Nothing but a bush. Instead, in the direction of the light on the horizon was an extremely bright half-moon, shining nonchalantly in the cloudless sky, none the wiser it was about to be attacked. The flickering was leaves and branches moving in the wind in front of it. I burst out laughing. How could I have got that so wrong? I was quite literally howling at the moon. Maybe I was turning into Teen Wolf. (Apologies to my younger readers, you may not get that reference from the 1980s.)

Chuckling away, I zipped my tent back up and nodded off, thinking how I may tell this story to my future grandkids: the night Grampa Gandalf – the name I'd like to be called, and yes, I will walk around with a staff – tried to scare away the moon with his feeble roar.

As night's sleep go it wasn't one of the best but that didn't matter because today was a big day. Today I'd be entering my favourite part of England, the idyllic Lake District. I first discovered this corner of England when I cycled Land's End to John O'Groats in 2008. I had lived in London for nearly 6 years and had never been north of Manchester. I remember coming over the hill from Kendal, huffing and puffing away, my legs killing me and then stopping dead in my tracks as I saw the beautiful Lake Windermere spread out before me, shafts of light pin-pricking through the clouds with Coniston Old Man covered in Snow in the distance. It was just as I had imagined it as a child reading books like, the Secret Garden and all Beatrix Potter's books. I was hooked. At the time I hadn't quite realised how drawn I was to the Lakes, and it took nearly another 10 years for me to finally give way to that ever growing force, pulling me towards mountains and water, two things I need in life.

After a brief stop in Penrith, I detoured west towards Haweswater, a reservoir due north-east of Lake Windemere. The best route for me to at least be able to say I went through the Lakes was to get to the south side of the reservoir, climb over the pass and run down into the Kentmere valley. Although the climb would only take about an hour, it was by far the most adventurous section I'd run since the West Highland Way (if you ignore my experience in Larkhall, obviously). The remoteness, altitude, potential gale force winds, ever changing weather and slippery surfaces all adding to my nervousness - especially as I had to do the section in road shoes which were worn smooth since Glasgow.

'Seano, my man. Damn you're looking thin. Come let me make you lunch!' shouted Ben as he ran towards me, just north of Bampton Grange. Ben is my friend Charlie's husband, and they had just moved up to the Lake District. It was good to have a running buddy, though slightly depressing when I realized just how slow I was.

We ran for about an hour along the back roads, enjoying the way the light falls across the stonewalled, sheep dotted fields, even though I had to jump up to see over the stone walls that were taller than I am to look at something that Ben was explaining to me. Jumping was not easy, but I wanted to save face so did it anyway. We reached Ben and Charlie's cottage, where we stopped and Ben made me the biggest spag-boll I've ever had, which was a godsend.

'Mate, thanks so much for coming to run with me. Which way to Haweswater?'

'What you mean? I'm coming with you.'

'Really? I'm going to go over the pass down to Kentmere and Staveley.'

'I'm right there with you man. Let's go.'

Ben's excitement was infectious and before long we were running down the east side of the reservoir.

'See all the stone walls running straight into the water? There is a village in there.'

'Really?'

'Yup! There used to be a village called Mardale Green, but in the 1930s Manchester needed more water, so they decided to extend Haweswater, which then turned this little hamlet into the Lakes District's own Atlantis.'

Apparently the church was dismantled piece by piece and the stones were used to build the water take off tower that we could just see on the other side of the reservoir as we ran past. The rest of the buildings were blown up by the Royal Engineers, although you can still see their remains when the water level gets unusually low.

The climb up the pass got windier and winder with every meter we climbed. The wind was blowing at around 50 mph coming from the south, which means we were in the shadow of its full force, the mountain protecting us. We knew that as soon as we reached the summit, we'd have no protection and I'd need to seriously watch my footing for fear of being blown over with my smooth shoes.

Ben was like a jack rabbit or whatever the British version is of someone who can run full speed ahead, with what seems to be no fear at all. A fell runner I guess is what we call them. The Lake District is famous for the fell running scene, which I think is the most wonderful of activities. It is one of the last uncommercial sports left in the world. The sport's understated heroes, like Billy

Bland, Joss Naylor, Bill Smith and Bob Graham, didn't become big stars or appear on the covers of magazines like many sports people of today. They just carried on with their everyday lives shearing sheep and milking goats or whatever, all the while being able to run unimaginable miles with awe-inspiring speed, grace and precision, both on the up hills, and more impressively, the downhills.

I could tell Ben had most certainly gained some pretty impressive experience on these hills as he effortlessly pounced along, placing each foot with complete confidence that it would hold its grip on the wet stones. I didn't dare try to copy him so rather hobbled down like the old man I felt. We had made it over the pass uninjured and started the slow slippery shuffle against a mind numbingly strong and cold headwind. Ben was way ahead of me making it all look too easy. That annoyed me. By the time I reached him at the bottom he was already shivering as he had been there for so long waiting for me.

'My knees just don't have it in them.' I said, not wanting to blame my inappropriate footwear. I hate it when people moan about how they could have done something better if they had the right equipment.

'Maybe so, but I have home turf advantage. Call it even.' Ben joked.

'No chance, you had me before that second sheep. Even on a good day I'd have been way back.'

'Come on. Four miles to go before the pub.'

Moments later a car pulled up beside me.

'Sean! I finally found you. I didn't know which route you were taking. I've brought tea.'

It was my friend Bruce who lived just down the road. He had said weeks earlier that he was going to try and come and see me but as I hadn't heard from him, I figured he was away doing epic stuff. He once hand-built a wooden canoe. It took him an almost unimaginable number of man hours to build, and was a thing of pure beauty. However in the end it ended up being too small for him so he can't use it. Gutted.

'Nice one mate. Thanks for the tea but I really need an ale. Meet you at the pub?'

'Sure thing. See you there.'

Just before we got to the pub, Ben said that we were about 30 miles from Penrith. I couldn't quite believe it, but if true, as I had started the day in the wood four miles on the other side of the town, it meant that today I would have run a mind blowing – my mind anyway – 34 miles. Just over a week ago this seemed completely impossible. It's amazing what the human body can do when it's not pooing itself to death.

Bruce parked up and met us in the small town of Staveley just down the valley. I needed to stock up on supplies for the morning before the shops closed. Ben said he'd go ahead and get the beers in while Bruce kept me company as I perused the aisles of Spar for the foodstuffs with the perfect carb/fat/protein mix. Having bought just enough so I was happy I had enough rations but not too much so I weighed down my rucksack I went over to the till.

My wallet. Where's my wallet? I checked my hip bag where I usually keep it. And I say wallet, but to save weight it is actually a small zip lock bag.

'Are you sure it's not in your pocket?' asked Bruce.

'No mate. I always keep in in my stupid American fanny pack.'

'Don't worry, I'll pay for your supplies buddy. I'm sure you'll find it.'

Bruce kindly paid for my snacks and we wandered towards the Eagle and Child Inn, just over a wonderfully tiny ye olde bridge, only wide enough for one car at a time – a navigational nightmare for tourists and Londoners I imagined. I stopped and took a quick photo and then staggered in to find Ben at the bar. It saddened me to find out that not long after I ran over that bridge huge floods washed it away. It took nearly two years before they were able to build it again.

Ben, Bruce and I all sat down to celebrate the biggest running day of my life, but annoyingly I couldn't relax. I was constantly worried about my wallet. It only had around £30 cash in it, but it also contained my only bank card. I couldn't realistically go any further without it, and waiting for another card to arrive would take up to five days. I had no ID either. I also hated the idea of borrowing money. I've always hated it. My dad taught me many things, but the two earliest lessons I can remember was when I was messing around in his office one afternoon. Dad was busy doing Dad stuff when he picked up the phone to call his secretary over from the office next door.

'Hi Susan. Please could you go and give this to Andrew. I owe him.' Dad reached into his pocket and got out 50 cents (we were living in South Africa at the time). Fifty cents is worth about a quarter of a penny nowadays, and wasn't worth much more back then either.

'Sure. Where is he?' Susan asked.

'Up at the abattoir, we had a rhino poached yesterday and he's doing the post-mortem.'

'OK, I'll drive up on my lunch break.'

When Susan had left, I questioned Dad on why he bothered to return such a small amount which surely even Andrew had forgotten about. His reply was simple: 'Sean, always pay back what you owe, no matter how small. It's very important you do that. Promise me you'll always do that.'

'Yes I will, of course.'

I remember even back then thinking that it this borrowing malarkey seemed like a lot of hassle, considering he had the 50 cents in his pocket anyway. It would have been a lot easier if he just hadn't borrowed it in the first place.

As I was leaving the room to go climb the Marula tree outside his office he followed up with: 'And also never be late. It's very impolite to be late.'

Those are the earliest life lessons I can remember. Always pay back what you borrow, no matter how small (but it's a lot more hassle to borrow than it's worth) and never be late because it's impolite.

So when my 'wallet' still couldn't be found, and Ben offered to lend me £100, it seemed far too much for my little brain to deal with. I just couldn't enjoy my pint or meal in the pub, even though as pubs go, the Eagle and Child is one of the best around.

'Fancy a bed for the night mate? I only live a few miles up the road. I can give you a lift and drop you back here tomorrow,' offered Bruce.

The idea of a bed after the biggest running day of my life was one of the best things I've ever been offered – even better than when I got offered to stand in for the lead in a school play for the day because the other kid had chicken pox or something. My character would get to hold hands with Jemima Salter-Banister, the prettiest girl in my class, but I declined because I had a very important fort to build in the woods. Had I lived in Scotland however, I would have agreed and shortly after married Jemima at Gretna Green.

But however much I really wanted to sleep in a comfortable bed, I still had my rule – even though I was quickly realizing it was bollocks anyway – that I couldn't get any assistance from a vehicle and had to make it on my own two feet. I'd broken it once at the service station in the emergency badger bowel situation, and I really didn't want to do it again.

'Sorry mate, I'd love to, but I can't get a lift anywhere. It's my own stupid rule but I'm sticking to it. I'll just camp somewhere here.'

'OK, fair enough. Don't camp though. My office is just up the road. You can stay in the showroom if you want. You'll have to crash on the floor, but there is a shower and I'm sure that's better than what you've had so far,' Bruce laughed.

'Mate, that's amazing.' I immediately felt in a better mood and gulped down another Cumbrian Way ale.

I said goodbye to Ben, who was getting a taxi back home, and then trudged along in the rain to Staveley Mill Yard.

We wandered up into the Haglofs office and Bruce showed me the shower room and the best place to sleep, which was in between two curtain rails full of fancy coloured jackets. I took my backpack off and then my rain jacket and threw it on the floor. I heard something metallic clank. That's strange. I went and picked it up. There was something in the pocket. I unzipped it.

'You cannot be serious?' I exclaimed a little over-theatrically.

'It's your wallet isn't it?' Bruce said.

'Yup.'

'You muppet, and you ruined your evening worrying about it.'

'I know. I'm just knackered I guess. Brain don't work so good when I'm knackered.'

'Well, at least you got it. Now get some rest.'

I felt like such a plonker. Bruce hadn't even left the room before I was fast asleep, deciding to save my shower for the morning.

Cutting into the Lake District

Chapter 12 – Towpath Tales

So I felt like death, the mixture of ale and big miles a bit too much for my body to handle, but the confidence I got from my 34-miler the previous day and not, as it turned out, having lost my wallet, was enough to keep my spirits high as I made my way south-east towards Kendal and out of the Lake District. I hadn't quite gone far enough into the Lakes to really explore them, but I promised myself I would return one day and do it properly.

Soon after Kendal I'd turn directly south after my short stint heading east from Staveley. For the next part of my journey I wasn't going to be running on roads, nor over mountains, but alongside some of Britain's very many canals. There were certain parts of my route where I made it up, rather unsuccessfully at times, as I went along, but I always knew from the start that I wanted to do as many miles on the towpaths as possible, providing the canals went roughly in the direction I wanted to run. That bit I hadn't quite researched. Canals were flat, often had a good path and were traffic free, the ideal situation for me to claw back some big miles. England and Wales have over 2,000 miles of canals and riverways, and if I wanted to I could get from Kendal all the way to Bristol running on towpaths away from roads. I wasn't quite going to do the entire route on the famous waterways, as there would be far too many detours, but the next week or so should be easy running. Getting to Land's End on the 4th May was still a distant dream, but it was becoming more and more possible with every day as my legs slowly realized we were on a running mission and needed to sort themselves out.

It seemed a rather odd place for the Lancaster canal to start, or, if you're coming north, for it to stop: under a bridge on a tiny back road in the small hamlet of Tewitfield, just over the border in Lancashire. It looked like maybe the canal used to carry on further, and I later found out it used to go all the way into Kendal but due to leaking was closed off. Apparently some high powered folk tried to close the entire canal once but didn't succeed and I'm so glad they didn't. Canals are the arteries of Britain from yesteryear and are an important part of our past, just like an old building, and should be conserved for their historical significance, as well as because they provide people with great opportunities for running, cycling and boating. (I am biased though as I live on a boat on a canal).

I had forgotten just how muddy some canal paths can be and immediately regretted getting road shoes in Glasgow. It was the type of mud that as a kid in bare feet would squish up in between your toes. I remember loving that feeling. It's one of the many things we as adults don't experience much anymore. I almost wanted to just take my shoes off and do it right there, but I needed to get some miles under my belt and it would probably not be a great idea anyway (see 'Body Management' in Sean Conway's patented five-point system for endurance adventure – you've got to have good foot care, people). So I promised myself that when I got home I'd look for mud to walk in with bare feet, to go between my toes again.

At this moment, however, I really needed some trail shoes with some heavy grip. All the pace and distance I should have gained from being on the flat towpath was erased by my horse-on-ice impersonation every 100 metres. The going was slow, and probably hilarious to watch.

I hadn't gone more than a few miles when the canal just decided to stop, right up against the M6 motorway. I looked on the map and it suggested the canal went underneath the road and carried on the other side but sadly this was not the case. I really didn't want to turn back, so my only option was some gentle trespassing across a farmer's field onto a fairly busy A-road for longer than I would have wished for. I hoped this wouldn't be a regular scenario as it was slowing me down. Eventually, after about an hour, I was back on the canal pretending to be an ice skating horse again.

'Hey mate. You're looking strong,' said Jez. He and Echo the dog were waiting for me on the towpath.

Jez, if you remember, was the skipper for the first half of Swimming Britain and bought the boat *Friday While* off me at the end, the one I stayed on in Fort William. He said he wanted to come and join me on his bicycle with his dog Echo – a beautiful Lurcher cross, and today was the day he had managed to come up from London.

The miles slipped away as Jez and I relived tales from the first few months of swimming Britain, and talked about just how lucky we were to get away with it. In hindsight, we were pretty gung-ho, with that sort of recklessness you only ever see in the young, or desperate people. I was both of them.

At 32 years old, I felt I still wanted to prove to myself what I was capable of. The swim was my way of saying to myself, 'Screw it Sean, you can do more than you think you can, you just have to really, really, want it.' The crew and I really did want it and Jez in particular had the same 'we can bloody do this' attitude as I did: he even quit his job to join the swim.

Those early days were like no other as we completely winged it, as none of us, myself included, had the faintest idea what we were in for – which was probably a good thing. Ignorance is bliss.

Echo was the most hyperactive dog I had ever seen. For every mile we ran, Echo must have done at least three as she pounded up and down chasing mice and frightening ducks.

Towards the end of the day, the canal went too far off course for us, so we detoured onto the busy A6. It was far less scenic but it was at least much more direct. Miles, miles, miles; I had to think of the miles – the harsh reality from having far too many toilet breaks at the beginning of the run, putting me behind schedule.

It was evening by the time we reached Carnforth and looked for a pub to settle in. A pub called The Canal Turn seemed the most inviting – and appropriate, considering we'd what we'd been doing all day.

'Ha ha! Look at the pub sign,' laughed Jez.

'No way! That is hilarious.'

I'd thought The Canal Turn was a perfectly named place for our evening meal, but someone had decided to vandalize the pub sign by getting rid of the 'c' in 'canal', which actually made the pub even more appropriate, considering the last few weeks I'd had.

After a long drawn out evening of a few too many Guinnesses and some woefully bad games of snooker, we headed out into the darkness in search of a place to camp. The closest thing we could find was a football pitch on the other side of the canal. It had been a good day. I have no idea how many miles I ran but was feeling strong.

'Wakey, wakey,' I heard a man shout, right next to my tent. Echo immediately growled from Jez's tent next door and I heard footsteps hurrying away. Coward!

It was 6.03am. As annoyed as I was by my rude awakening, it was nice to get up a little earlier for a change. Actually, it was a good thing we did get up a little early as dealing with a hungry dog takes up rather a lot of time of a morning. Eventually, by 7.15am, we were running past the Canal Turn pub and back on the towpath.

Bolton-le-Sands was the next village we came across. I know what you're thinking. The 'le' in Bolton-le-Sands must date from the Norman invasion 1,000-odd years ago, when the French thought to put their own stamp on English towns, and it has stuck ever since. This is true for many places, however Bolton-le-Sands decided to add the 'le-Sands' part less than 200 years ago. I do like the idea of a town council meeting whereby they were deciding on this:

'Rupert, we need to make Bolton more exotic, more inspiring, and more cultural perhaps. Let's add some French flair to it,' (honestly, this Rupert guy finds his way into all my imaginary conversations) and so it became Bolton-le-Sands. The actual Bolton of today was called Bolton-le-Moors, but they decided to get rid of the 'le-Moors', which is a shame in my opinion, but maybe that's why I've never been asked to name a town.

The canal continued south and we all fell into a rhythm. I hobbled along while Jez cycled ahead trying in vain to make Echo do less mileage. If I ran a marathon today then it'd be quite easy for Echo to run around 40–50 miles, although I hoped that when she started to get tired she'd keep to heel. However, that seemed unlikely, considering her levels of boundless energy.

'She sometimes runs alongside me on the bike with a lead on, but she's capable of pulling me sideways, and I don't fancy a swim today,' Jez laughed.

I secretly wished he would do that. Jez falling in the canal would be without doubt the funniest thing since the Anal Turn.

It's a bit surprizing that Jez has a dog, because when he was in his twenties he was attacked by one and it bit off his ear. Jez now only has one ear. I've asked him before about getting another one put on and he said that he once went to the NHS to get it sorted but they were too busy doing boob jobs, so he gave up. Also, Jez just doesn't give two hoots about appearances and social norms. I think that's why we get along.

Lunch was in a pub in Lancaster before hitting the canal again towards Garstang. A little while after lunch I said goodbye to Jez and Echo as they veered off to the nearest train station and I continued south towards Preston.

As I got nearer Preston, every road was flanked by rows of houses. I faced the usual conundrum when entering a more built up area of a lack of places to camp. Ordinarily I'd have skipped a big city like this but I needed to cross the River Ribble, which comes in from the west, and the centre of Preston was my best option for this.

Other than Glasgow, which I had a reason to go through to get new shoes, I really hadn't had to deal with cities much and was still finding my feet when it came to town logistics. If I had been a little more prepared I would have tried to do a few extra miles each day in the lead up, which meant I could have got through Preston and camped on the other side. It's not a very big city, and so it really wouldn't have needed to be a lot – maybe four or five miles, and I'd have been in the clear, on the other side, camping next to a fence with a disgruntled cow in a field next to mine. Sadly I wasn't that organized and it was now 9pm and I was just approaching the northern bypass that runs west towards Blackpool.

I started to reconcile myself to the fact that I would probably have to resort to my weekly allowance of a hotel for the night – I had hoped to save my night of luxury for somewhere near Manchester. With my head hung low I found the nearest hotel and passed out naked on the bed while my clothes were drying on the radiator after their second soak in free miniature shampoo. At least my Two and a Quarter Rule was back to zero now, so I had a chance of meeting future Mrs Conway Hemingway.

I often get caught up in the moment, in life generally. I'm very easily influenced (and not that organized, as you have seen), so when my Uncle Gavin and Aunty Trish said: 'You're going to stop by when you do your run aren't you? We'll stock you up on biltong.' I got very, very excited. Biltong is probably my favourite snack in the world. I must give fair warning to all my vegan friends, you may want to skip this next bit, because biltong is a traditional South African meat that has been covered with herbs and spices and hung to cure and dry out for a few days. If you go to any event in South Africa – a wedding, dinner party, BBQ, whatever – there will always be a plate of sliced biltong and it will most certainly be the first plate to be finished. The thought of Uncle Gavin's homemade biltong literally sent tingles down my belly – not to mention that there is 50g of protein per 100g of meat, twice that of chicken or steak. So obviously I said, 'Yes, of course I'll swing by.'

The one thing I failed to really comprehend was actually where Gav and Trish lived – Macclesfield. This was probably a day off course and meant I would probably have to run through Manchester to get there. Luckily, Gavin's biltong is worth running through the centre of the third biggest city in England for.

The centre of Preston to the centre of Manchester was pretty much a day's run so it was likely I'd end up having to stay another night in a hotel. I was certainly going to have to do some serious wild camping from now on to bring myself back to reality. All these soft beds and clean clothes would make me weak, and nothing good comes from that when trying to run 1,000 miles carrying everything you need to live.

To make city running more exciting, I came up with a new game. I called it Zombie Chicken. This was the first time on my journey that I had run through the central part of town at rush hour when the pavements were full of people hastily walking to work. Almost everyone had their head down doing something on their phones – something that was obviously so important it would change the world. The game was to choose someone ahead who was coming towards me and would move directly into their path and then stop, to see if anyone actually walked into me.

Player number one in the inaugural game of Zombie Chicken was an older chap, the kind that you'd expect to not have a mobile phone at all. However, he was in zombie mode seven or maybe eight – ten being the most zombie. He was wearing headphones and seemed to be watching something on his phone, laughing briefly. He was a good twenty meters away but I was strangely nervous, even though technically I was probably always going to win, because, well, that often happens when the other competitor doesn't know he's actually in a game.

Ten metres and he still hadn't looked up.

Five metres . . .

Four metres . . .

Three metres . . .

I wanted to jump aside, but surely he wasn't going to walk in to me?

Then at two metres he briefly looked up, nonchalantly moved aside and looked back down at his phone, passing me to my right.

'Yesssss!' I said under my breath, kind of.

'Sorry?' the man took his one headphone out and looked at me as if he thought I was talking to him.

'Ah. Nothing mate. Have a good day!' I replied in that sort of crazy person way again.

I was 1–0 up and my next contestant was already in front of me: a young woman, in her late twenties I guessed, frantically texting away. I moved in front of her with fifteen meters to go and held my ground. She was walking at quite some pace mind.

Ten metres . . .

Five metres . . .

She showed no signs of looking up.

Three metres . . .

Two metres . . .

She was almost on top of me; my heart was racing.

One metre . . .

She still hadn't looked up. I couldn't take the pressure and jumped aside.

'Sorry,' I said overly politely, as if it were my fault.

'You're weak you are, weak! Can't believe you lost a game with a girl who didn't even know she was playing,' said Little Flying Cow.

It was true. Maybe the night in the hotel wasn't a good idea.

I continued running through Preston getting better and better at Zombie Chicken and in the end the score was 11–3 to me. With my confidence restored I left rush hour zone and continued south east towards Manchester.

Considering today was all about cities, I figured I should probably go and visit the other Bolton, formerly part of the famous Bolton-le-Moors parish, to try and work out why they dropped the 'le-Moors' from the title.

The road opened out and I started climbing up alongside Darwin Moor. It was nice to be out the hustle and bustle of the city, even if I did have a cracking headwind.

By the time I reached Bolton I was starving, and experience has taught me to always get food at the first option I came across. More often than not, if you skip it you won't see another place again, and I hate going back on myself. Bolton's first food establishment was a chippy. Not the most nutritious, but calories are calories.

'Do you know why Bolton dropped the "le"?' I asked the Chippy man. He looked at me blankly.

'What "le"?' he replied somewhat confused.

'Bolton. This area used to be the Bolton-le-Moors parish but they dropped the "le-moors" bit.'

'Right.' He looked blankly again. 'That's £5.95, mate.' This seemed a clear indication he wanted me out of the shop. I left fairly unhappy with both my meal and my progress in getting to the bottom of things.

I asked a further six people as I wandered through town but not one single person had any clue of the previous name. It was then I realized I had become that crazy person. Like the one who walks down the street asking people about when the aliens are coming. I decided to leave Bolton-le-Moors hastily.

Manchester was on the horizon and not far beyond, on the other side, a huge pile of biltong was waiting for me. This, and my newfound love for Zombie Chicken, was the only way I was able to cope with the marauding crowds and succession of traffic lights.

The afternoon flew by as I kept my head down. By 10pm I had reached Manchester and settled into my hotel and fallen fast asleep dreaming of Zombies taking over the world.

Since the start of the run I hadn't really slept that much, but today was the day where I did just that. Thank you black out blinds. I awoke at around 9.30am and felt like a new man, even though I had missed breakfast in the hotel, and I can assure you, I never miss a free breakfast for anyone.

The going was slow through Manchester but I eventually came out the other side in one piece. For the third day in a row I ran into the night. I was hoping that it was because I was getting stronger and able to run for longer, but it was more likely that I was just running slower and needed more time to cover the distance. I had stopped recording my daily miles a while back, as it made me rather depressed and instead decided to just run until I was tired, or found a nice pub. This was a hard decision to make because I was so dead set on my marathon a day target but in the end, it was taking the focus away from the adventure. I said to myself I would give 110% each day, not an ounce less. If that wasn't enough then I'd just have to make peace with the fact I wasn't born to be a runner. I therefore decided to just see what my mileage was at the end of every other day to give me at least an idea of where I was, rather than staring at my milometer every minute trying to work out the maths to see if I was doing well or not.

Tonight was no exception. The internet told me that three miles ahead there was a rather fancy pub with 4.5-star rating. I usually try and avoid these posh pubs because the same calories usually cost double the price and I sadly didn't have the luxury of choosing food for its taste, but rather how fatty and salty it is. Nevertheless, it's nice to treat yourself once in a while.

I climbed over the final stone wall and followed the last bit of public footpath towards the pub, deeply in thought about what meal – and when I say meal, I really mean steak – I was going to order when I suddenly heard a quick, harsh, heavy snort to my left. I looked up and the world's biggest horse was coming right for me at pace. Now, I'm not really afraid of much really, except balloons that have the potential to pop near me, and champagne corks, but I do get somewhat nervous around horses. I mean, they are huge, and have huge teeth. My fear doesn't extend to other animals that you can ride, like donkeys, camels, elephants or rhinos. (Yes, I have ridden a rhino. It was an orphaned one that had become a pet because we couldn't reintroduce it into the wild as both its parents had been poached when it was very young.) So I don't know why horses bother me. They always seem to look at me funny. My mum tells me my fear probably comes from when I was a child and a horse tried to eat my hair, thinking it was some hay. The curse of ginger hair continues. Also *probably*, Mum? I'd say *definitely*. How would you like it if you were nearly decapitated by a horse when you were five years old?

The killer horse was just five metres away. I have never run so fast in my entire life. I dared not look back and clambered over the other wall and back onto the road. Five minutes later I was sat at the bar, toasting to my near-death experience and giving the couple sitting next to me the full blow-by-blow account. They were on a date and the bloke was giving me a look that said, 'Stop interfering with my romantic evening, mate. We don't want to talk to a wandering smelly nomad about killer horses.' But I finished my story anyway.

'Howzit cousin. You've done well, said Duncan as we met up the following morning.

Duncan is my first cousin, Uncle Gav and Trish's son, and he also lives in Macclesfield. He decided to take the morning off work to come and run the ten miles into town with me. It had been ages since we last saw each other.

We followed the main road for a while, past some pretty impressive Cheshire mansions, before cutting through some boggy fields for no other reason than I thought Duncan's shoes looked a bit clean and needed to get muddied. You only become a real trail runner when you can't tell the colour of your shoes – or, whether you even have shoes on at all. It's a bit like my mother used to say about riding: 'You're not a real horse rider until you get bloodied.' My horse fear has literally just made sense to me as I write this. Thanks Mum!

It was a few hours before I could smell the distinct waft of raw dried beef coming from Uncle Gav's shed.

'Sean! Well done, boy.'

'Thanks Gav. I tell you, I could have done with your biltong a few weeks ago.'

'Agg man, you should have said. I'd have posted you some,' laughed Gavin in his familiar Rhodesian accent.

'I know, but I needed something to look forward to hey.' I replied, finding myself slipping into the accent myself, although I was technically born in Zimbabwe as it was after the name change in 1979. I don't know what it would be like now, but back then it was pretty hard for the rest of the world to understand when a country changes its name. For a while, Zimbabwe just didn't exist as a country at many airports, which made life quite interesting for my parents who tried to get into America from Canada in 1980. You can just imagine.

'Excuse me sir, madam. Your passport says Zimbabwe but that isn't on my list. Is this passport for real?' As the man slowly slips on a rubber glove.

'No sir, we are from Zimbabwe, but it used to be called Rhodesia.'

'Well, it does not say Rhodesia, it says Zimbabwe, which isn't on the list madam.'

This went on for an ridiculous amount of time, as you can imagine, and in 1980 you couldn't just say 'Google it, you nitwit'.

Eventually someone with common sense, a Mexican probably, understood the situation and they got through without any invasive rubber glove treatment and had a wonderful time in America, as most people do once they've made it through the criminal style interrogation you often get at American airports.

After five cups of tea and loaded down with about three-and-a-half days' worth of protein, I said my goodbyes and headed off. I don't often get to see this side of my family, so it was nice to catch up, and especially to hear about my other cousin Gordon who was away working on some oilrigs in Vietnam. And the diversion was totally worth it for all the biltong of course.

I was back on the canals in no time, which was a welcome break after days on main roads since Jez and Echo left. I could finally put both headphones in (I only use one headphone when running on main roads so I can hear the traffic) and I chose some orchestral rock music to keep my legs moving.

The plan was to use the Shropshire Union Canal to Birmingham and then pick up the Birmingham and Worcester Canal all the way to my houseboat, which was moored near Worcester. A night at home was just what I needed, and although it was still four days away it was something to aim for and was helping keep my spirits high.

After a few hours I swapped the canals for a beautiful trail running alongside an old railway line from Rushton Spencer to Rudyard. There's something magical about these old tracks and how they were built. I imagined all the hustle and bustle and wondered why it all came to an end. Maybe it was as a result of the Beeching cuts of the 1960s or maybe there was another reason. This sad railway line probably stood abandoned for decades before someone had the sense to convert it into a footpath, and I'm so glad they did.

Deep in thought about things I promised myself I needed to learn more about, like the Industrial Revolution and how much it would cost to make my very own train line, I plodded on and made good mileage well into the night. I was starting to love the long evening runs, which were often preceded by a long pub meal, a couple of ales (for extra calories of course) and Wilson deep in my ass. I'd become something of a pro at humping the little bugger. I could even do it in full sight on a pub chair without anyone even having a clue. Life goals!

These night sessions brought with them a sense of calm. I liked the idea that everyone is at home living their lives while I got to have the canals all to myself, for the most part. Weirdly, I also figured out that I ran about a mile an hour faster. Much later I realized the reason for this was that I'd keep my head down at night, because there was nothing to see, and this would mean my body position was leant forward, which would make me run faster. I'm pretty sure this is the normal way to run but it turns out my style has become quite arched backwards over time. I think this must be because I have never once run a marathon without at least a 7kg rucksack, often 10kg, pulling the top of my spine backwards. So I now have a very weird running style even when I take the rucksack off and it takes all the concentration in the world to run normally and not look like I'm going to fall on my arse.

By 11pm I had found a small actual campsite and settled into my coffin tent for the night, refuelled with 50g of protein from Uncle Gavin's biltong. It was nice to have a night not having to worry about the wild camping spy drones finding me.

Despite my newly invented immature game making city running a bit more fun, I really didn't feel like the faff of Birmingham. Luckily, according to my workings, it looked like I'd only get to Birmingham late the next night, thus avoiding the evening rush hour. If I got up ridiculously early the following day I'd avoid the morning rush hour too.

'Why don't you just run through the city at midnight? It'll be really quiet and you will miss all of the rush hours?' suggested Little Flying Cow.

My heart raced, as it always does with exciting new ideas, and this was a quite possibly the best brainwave Little Flying Cow had ever had (he's normally so unhelpful). If I ran through Birmingham in the early hours of the morning then it'd be quiet and surely save me loads of time.

I still had to get through today without incident, though. Any delay and I wouldn't make Birmingham, and I'd be forced to do it the day after, in the morning, with hordes of Zombies on their phones slowing me down. Game on.

Spring was now in full swing and my cold mornings would soon be nothing but a long, distant memory. This new, easier, less aggressive way of life was very welcome and I felt I needed to do a little dance or something to show the smug gods I was grateful. I say 'aggressive', because looking back to the first few weeks it seemed everything was constantly trying to kill me: Scotland, radioactive sand, snow, wind, my broken gut, all relentlessly out to get me. Now that those days were well behind me I was starting to enjoy the run.

Yes, my hamstring was still sore (which I also later found out was due to my over arched back pinching a nerve), and I still had to do a ridiculous mileage each day, to try and beat Eddie Izzard, but the weather was good, the rapeseed fields were in full bloom and I hadn't had stomach issues in days. The weather was so good in fact, and set to stay that way, that I could start to think about getting rid of some of my cold weather kit. I really wanted to stop right there and throw everything out that I didn't need but I thought I'd do it in the morning – something to look forward to and all.

I wandered right into the Blithfield Hall grounds, a very impressive private estate near Stafford that has been in the Bagot family since the fourteenth century. I love Britain for these sort of things. Imagine having that family history around you for your whole life. It must have an effect on your decisions, how you perceive things, philosophy and what's important in the world. It would be a very interesting way of growing up; knowing that generations before you have been tied down to one building, one location, and I guess the pressure to stay there and carry on the family tradition must be enormous. It's impossible for me, and pretty much every other person in the world, to fathom this sort of existence. I for example have lived in around thirty different homes, in three countries in my life. I can't imagine only having ever lived in one, even if this one was bigger than all thirty of mine added together. I do wonder if the Bagot family would get bored and move to a different wing of the house every 10 years or so, for a change and all. I'm not sure moving from one side of the manor to the other side counts as moving house even though you probably would still need to rent a removal truck.

Other than owning an impressive pile of bricks, the Bagot family is arguably more renowned for having their own breed of goat, the Bagot goat. The goats are white with black heads and necks, and they've lived semi-wild around the grounds of the house for hundreds of years. This tickled me a lot. I can't decide if it's grounds for immediate mockery, or just very, very cool. If there was a Conway goat I'd be made up. I'd have stamps printed, posters, a visitor's centre and the goat would have its own coat of arms. I've always dreamt of being that crazy old man in the village, who drives his tribe of goats down the high street because, well, there is a 1,200 year old bylaw that says I can. I guess I had better start breeding goats now then.

Sadly there are less than 200 breeding females left in the Bagot goat flock, which means the breed is recognised as 'vulnerable' by the Rare Breeds Survival Trust. It would be very sad if they did die out, one less wonderful British eccentricity lost by the wayside in our modern, often disposable existence.

After a less than peaceful sleep in a secluded woodland I was awake, having set my alarm for an hour earlier than usual, because today was the day I'd hopefully make Birmingham. It was also the day for a full blown spring clean. The goal was to try and get rid of two pounds of weight. This excited me no end as I took everything out of my rucksack and fanny pack and sprawled it all over the grass.

The first thing that needed to go were my gloves. They weighed at least 150g, and probably double that when wet. Then my knee tape and the knee brace. I hesitated briefly as I was most certainly tempting fate but decided to risk it anyway and get rid of them too. Then the extra Imodium, (I really was tempting fate), my second bandanna (I kept one of them as a neck scarf for sunburn mainly), my knee warmers, half my pack of baby wipes, which I used to give myself a full morning wash which I can tell you was a huge luxury as I had been limiting my use to one or maybe two a day up till that point. I was very tempted to get rid of my down jacket but thought that was one tempting fate item too many and decided to roll it up really tight and put it right at the bottom of my pack.

I also figured all the 1p and 2p coins that had collected at the bottom of my bag were weighing me down, so I figured I'd leave them in places for people to find. I decided that I would put them on top of the pedestrian button at a traffic light, so when a Zombie was head down in a rush for work and got to a red light they'd be annoyed, then see the penny and think, 'Oh look, a lucky penny.' Which hopefully, for a brief moment at least, would bring them out of Zombie mode. I'm a dreamer I know.

I left the campsite with a new spring in my step. I had hoped to lose two pounds of weight but in reality, it was probably only around one pound. And of course, I couldn't really feel the weight loss at all, but the thought that it was lighter was good enough.

This new idea of running through a deserted city was just what my knees wanted to hear. The slower I ran today with more breaks, the later I'd get to Birmingham. By early morning it was already baking hot, immediately giving me a certain smugness about my spring clean. I carried on along the canal towpaths, which allowed me to switch off, listen to music if I wanted, and get the miles under my belt.

Because today was going to be a longer day I thought it was a good time to get another massage. There were four massage parlours – sorry, clinics – along my route. I worked out that I'd reach the first one at midday, the second at around 1pm, the third at 4pm and the last one at around 4.30pm. I didn't want to have to wait around for hours so, in an unprecedented feat of organization, I called each one to see which could fit me in at the exact time I would arrive. The 1pm chap could see me at 1.15pm for a 45-minute beating, which was perfect.

The morning dragged on as I clock-watched till I arrived at just after 1pm. The next 45 minutes of my life were possibly the most painful I have ever experienced. All 700 or so miles of knots and tightness gave a pretty good fight as Ryan dug his elbow deep into my thigh. I now also know why many sportsmen shave their legs: it really hurt when he went deep and ran down my thigh, pulling the hair out. I'm still never going to shave my legs though.

The suburbs of Birmingham gave way to bigger and bigger buildings as the night drew in. My pace increased slightly while I spread my load of 1p and 2p coins at every traffic light until they were gone.

By midnight I was nearing the city centre, and it was 1am when I eventually plodded down Broad Street. What a different experience. It was eerily quiet. Well, other than a few drunk people shouting 'Oi Oi. Look, it's Forrest Gump. Weeeeeeeey!' as I ran past. Lads!

By 2am I had reached the other side of Birmingham and I settled into the first cheap hotel I could find that had a 24-hour reception. The chap checking me in didn't quite know what to make of me as I struggled to write my name and fake email address on his form.

I then settled in to wash my clothes, something I was needing to do far more regularly than before now the weather was warming up to keep within the Two and a Quarter rule.

Finally some easy, traffic-free, flat paths to run on

Chapter 13 – Sweet Smell of Home

I could almost smell home. I know all canals probably smell the same, but somehow today's stench of rotting algae and swan poo smelled exactly like the canal outside my boat. I loved it. I hadn't quite thought about the fact I was running home and getting to sleep in my own bed. This is something I normally only ever did at the end of a journey, not half way through. I wonder if my body would presume I had finished and kind of give up? It was certainly going to be strange having to get up the next day to carry on, leaving all my home comforts behind.

To keep me entertained I decided to invent another game; it would be called Chasing Ducks. When I cycled around the world I invented a game called Chasing Dogs, where I tried to see how far I could get a barking dog to run away from its owner (hopefully without catching up with me!) if the owner hadn't shown any remorse for letting his unruly hound chase me down the road. It was a fine art. Cycle too fast and the dog loses interest very quickly, cycle too slowly however, and you get bitten, as I experienced in Peru when a little snapper caught me on the ankle. My record was I think around 500 meters I seem to remember, but I get a bit hazy on the details of that bike ride now, even though it was only six years ago. People that say all you take to the grave are memories have obviously never hung out with me - my memory is awful.

Chasing Ducks was a similar game. However, I would be doing the chasing. The goal was to see how far I could get ducks to swim along the canal away from me before they either turned around or flew off. I'm not sure I had much control in this game but I played it with childish enthusiasm anyway.

By the time I neared Worcester I had got my Chasing Duck distance to around 41 meters. That didn't feel very far at all, and I was annoyed that I had spent all day creeping up on ducks, looking like a crazy person, all for 41 meters. I needed to change my strategy, but that was for another day because I was nearly home. Home sweet home.

In 2013, while I was swimming Britain, I saw a 1931 Second World War Pinnace for sale on eBay for £2,000. She was called *Lady Sybil* and she was the most beautiful boat I had ever seen. Sadly she had fallen into disrepair – as you can imagine you do not get a lot of working boat for £2,000, especially considering she is 56ft long. She was in a right mess and probably should have been scrapped, but I fell in love instantly. I then spent the next three years painstakingly doing her up. She is my pride and joy.

No matter how good a job you do with the hull, any wooden boat owner will tell you there is always that slight worry that it will spring a leak and the boat will sink. I put five automatic bilge pumps (pumps that turn on automatically when water gets into the boat) on *Lady Sybil* and moored her on a part of the canal where the bottom was only a metre below the keel, so she couldn't go too far in any case. So I felt slightly nervous as I ran down the towpath until I finally saw her distinctive chimney flue towering over all the other boats around her. She was still there and looking more beautiful than ever in the evening light.

As I opened her door I was hit with that wonderful smell of wood and engine bay that you get on old teak boats. Some people hate the smell as it often is associated with dampness, but it was my damp and I loved it.

First task was to light a fire to warm her up and dry her out a little. Lady Sybil has two fire places, one in the saloon and one down below in my bedroom. I've said it before and I'll say it again: having a fireplace in your bedroom is pretty much the best thing in life. Words can't quite describe how peaceful and relaxing it is going to sleep with the gentle flicker of flames casting dancing shadows onto the walls while centimetres from your face, on the other side of the hull, two swans dance together in the moonlight. Boat life is just wonderful.

The only slight annoyance was that I had run out of gas a few days before I left for John O'Groats. At the time I remember thinking, 'Well it's not worth the effort to go all the way into town to get more gas before I leave. I'll sort it when I'm back.'

Planning not being my strong point meant I had no hot water for a shower, which was kind of annoying. At least I would get a shower tomorrow because I was going to stop at Mum's for the night in Cheltenham before heading down to Bristol where I had planned to meet a few people to run with me. A huge motivational factor in my run was to inspire people to get outdoors and get fitter. I realise I may have taken *fitness* to the extreme over the years and I'm not suggesting everyone tries to run the length of Britain, although I will suggest my future children do it one day. But getting more people active really does make me excited and spur me on when I'm tired. It's the simple tweets that read; 'Sean, seeing you run the length of Britain has made me realise I have no excuse not to do a 5k. Anyone who's done any sort of challenge can relate to this. It makes you feel all warm a fuzzy. To thank people for supporting me on this run I had arranged for people to come and run with me in Bristol in a few days time. Even if only one person turned up it was enough.

It was around 30 miles to Cheltenham to see Mum, where I would not only and have another night under the covers, but after nearly a month, I was going to be washing my clothes in an actual washing machine, with detergent. I hoped that clean clothes on top of all this comfortable bed malarkey wasn't making me soft, but I didn't care. I just really needed clean clothes.

I don't think I've ever been so excited about such a mundane task such as laundry before. My socks in particular were pretty darn disgusting. In fact, they were so dirty and sweat-sodden that I could almost hold them horizontal and they'd stay solid, like a sword. I even once, on day 23 I think, had a sword fight against a fern tree with my rock solid socks, and won. I do hope that's on some CCTV camera somewhere and being used for a security companies' marketing videos alongside the line: 'Humans are weird and unpredictable so get our surveillance cameras.'

I said goodbye to *Lady Sybil* and headed off down to the river to follow the Severn Way out of town. It was great to be back on home turf. I knew this section well. Luckily my legs, although stiff, hadn't forgotten the task at hand and hadn't decided to stay on the boat. It started off a bit muddy but not the fun toe mud, so I wasn't tempted to take my shoes off. The going was steady until about three miles south when it became completely overgrown with knee-high nettles. Not feeling in the Roman warrior mood, I diverted onto the quicker A38 which had a good pavement on it all the way to the Cheltenham turning.

My days had become perfectly spread out over the last week. I had been doing around 25–30 miles a day and had had two nights in a bed with a third waiting for me at Mum's. Today was day 35 and I had run around 800 miles. I knew the maths on this meant I was way behind schedule on daily average but I was feeling stronger than ever and still had time to claw back the miles and just about get to Land's End for the 4th May. It was going to be tight and I couldn't afford any disasters.

I was just feeling smug at my achievements and how smoothly things were going when I looked at my phone to see a tweet from my Welsh friend Matthew Pritchard. He was having a rant about how it wasn't right that I was 'running Britain' and not going via Wales.

Dammit he was right! I hadn't really even thought about it. What an oversight from my part. How on earth could I have called my adventure 'Running Britain' and not gone via Wales? Also, what about Northern Ireland? Is that in Britain or the United Kingdom? I, much like quite a lot of people I imagine, get confused about the difference between Great Britain, the United Kingdom and the British Isles. I have definitely researched this about a hundred times but I still get it all mixed up. If Britain did include Northern Ireland as well as Wales then I'd made an awful misjudgement. I took out my phone and hesitated before I started the search. I kind of didn't want to know the truth, if it wasn't in my favour.

I searched: What the difference between Britain, United Kingdom and the British Isles?

The first thing that came up was on the Ordnance Survey website which was very embarrassing because I was one of their Get Outside Champions. Why can I never make this information stay in my head? I thought. I have known, many times over, but I just didn't think to check until now. Anyhow, this is the answer:

The United Kingdom
The United Kingdom of Great Britain and Northern Ireland (to give its full name) refers to the political union between England, Wales, Scotland and Northern Ireland. The UK is a sovereign state,

but the nations that make it up are also countries in their own right.

From 1801 to 1922 the UK also included all of Ireland.

The Channel Islands and Isle of Man are not part of the UK, but are Crown Dependencies.

Great Britain

Great Britain is the official collective name of England, Scotland and Wales and their associated islands. It does not include Northern Ireland and therefore should never be used interchangeably with 'UK' – something you see all too often.

British Isles

This is purely a geographical term – it refers to the islands of Great Britain and Ireland – including the Republic of Ireland – and the 5,000 or so smaller islands scattered around our coasts. Remember this only refers to geography, not nationality, and while the Republic of Ireland is part of the British Isles, its people are not British – a very important distinction.

So luckily for me, 'Britain' does not include Northern Ireland and in fact only includes England, Scotland and Wales. So thanks to Matthew I realized I really needed to at least step onto Welsh soil once on this run. Thankfully I discovered this before I had gone past it.

Just then Matt sent another tweet enticing me over the border even more, in the only way he knows how: 'A rave around a campfire with whisky and loud music.'

That was quite the offer: whisky and campfires are another two of my favourite things, along with steak and nostalgia. So I was going to have to make a detour to Wales, and to keep on target for 4th May, it would mean I'd have to run over 40 miles – the biggest running day of my entire life. I'm not sure anyone has ever run 40 miles to have a pint with a Welshman, but the idea excited me a lot.

What didn't excite me so much was what might happen to me once I reached Wales, because my friend Matthew's previous job was to be as crazy as possible for a TV program. He was in an MTV show called *Dirty Sanchez*, which for all you American readers, if you're still here, was like *Jackass*, but in Wales. I remember seeing him back in those days, before we became friends, and thinking, 'What an idiot'. Why roll around in nettles completely bollock naked? Although that was before I knew of the nettle's historic uses. However, I'm almost certain Roman warriors didn't sting their manhood – not on purpose anyway.

So a pint with Mr Pritchard could very well mean waking up beardless in Bulgaria, but you only live once, and I've never been to Bulgaria, so Wales, here we come. Well, after I'd washed my clothes at Mum's. I wouldn't want to subject even Matt to my rotting socks.

The A38 was unremarkable and nothing much happened all afternoon as I kept dreaming about getting my clothes washed in an actual washing machine. I was 2 streets away when I caught a glimps of my reflection in a car window. I really looked a mess. I thought it's best I try and neaten up before seeing mum so I got my Swiss army knife out and trimmed the straggling hairs on my beard and moustache. In reality it made very little difference, I still looked a mess but at least I tried.

'Oh my boy, well done.' Mum said as she ran down the road towards me. She had been waiting at the front door looking down he street for me.

'Oh dear, you smell. You really smell my boy.' Mum pretended she wanted to vomit. At least I think it was pretend.

'Nice to see you too Mum,' I joked.

'Come, I've made dinner and bought extra washing powder and fabric softner.'

'Amazing. Exactly what I needed. I wasn't making any friends.'

'You mean you tried to make friend smelling like that?'

'Good point.' I replied, realising I had completely been waiting my time in any and all relationship based quests in the last few weeks. My stench as it turned out was way more disgusting than I had thought. You do get used to your own smell it seems, no matter how horrible it is.

It was great to be back at Mums for a well-earned break. She has been my number one fan since the beginning and has always supported me. No matter what stupid idea I come up with, she always says she loves it and immediately offers to help out. It was great spending the night catching up and getting a good feed.

By 9pm I was knackered so I said goodnight to Mum and went off to bed. My old room is at the back of the flat – a tiny single room with a bunk bed. Sleeping here brings up many mixed feelings. For over two years, from the age of 31, I lived in this little room, on this rickety bunk bed while I tried to make ends meet as that bearded swimming, cycling, running chap. When you really strive for your dreams, the trade-off is quite often personal finances. Many people speak about it. In fact, it's the email I get the most from people who are in a similar situation to what I was back then: How can you give it up and still pay your bills? My answer is always the same. If your dream means having to move back in with your parents to live on a bunk bed and you don't want to do that, then your dream isn't really a dream. Yes, I was fortunate enough to have a parent who was willing to let their 31-year-old son sleep in their spare room while he planned silly challenges, but even without this there are always ways of reducing your bills to free up time – which, after all, is the most valuable asset we all have.

Those few years with Mum were tough, probably more so for Mum than for me, but I had a vision. At first, the vision was more how I didn't want to live my life, rather than what I really wanted to do. I still don't really know today what I want out of life, but in the meantime I'm not going to settle. Instead I'm going to keep doing many different things until I eventually become the old man with a tribe of Conway goats, causing chaos on the high street.

With a smile on my face as I thought about my future life as a crazy shepherd, and listened to the beautiful hum of the washing machine cleaning my clothes for the first time in a month, I fell into a deep sleep.

Seeing sunrise and sunset every day was very rewarding

Chapter 14 – Welsh Detour

At 04.37 the sound of my alarm jolted me straight upright. I don't tend to set my alarm for 'obvious' times, which people sometimes find strange. It's not superstitious or anything. It's just something I've done for years. It's never on the hour or on five-minute intervals, like 5:05am or 5:10am, rather it's always at 5:03am or 5:06am. It's strange I know, but I feel like a rebel when I do it.

Slightly blurry eyed, I ducked my head to get off the bed – now a well-ingrained habit after many episodes of head-butting the ceiling. This was the earliest I had gotten up and my knees felt it. I was going to need all the jiggery-pokery in the world to get me 40 miles to the Welsh border in one piece. A sliver of good news though, was that after the back roads into Gloucester, I could hit the Gloucester and Sharpness Canal and then the Severn Way all the way to the old Severn Bridge where I'd cross over into Wales. The bad news was I was going to have to go back on myself slightly to get back onto the Severn Way. I think I was probably more annoyed by that than the fact I had to run 40 miles just to have a pint with a Welshman.

I said goodbye to Mum and she made me promise to get to Land's End on the 4th May because she'd taken the day off work already.

Within minutes I felt like a new man, full of energy, and I can only pinpoint it down to one thing - my new lavender-scented clothing. I couldn't believe I hadn't washed my clothes earlier. In fact, I felt certain they were about a pound lighter too with all the gunk and salt washed away. The fabric was flowing effortlessly through the air and gently flapping against my skin as I ran along. It felt wonderful. Right there, I promised myself I would clean my clothes at least once a week on any future adventures. It's been three years since I said that and as I write this I can honestly tell you I have not stuck to that at all. Sadly, that may be another end note to my gravestone: 'You could always smell him coming a mile off.'

The towpath south of Gloucester was the best I had been on. It was basically a small road at times and hard under foot which meant my pace was a steady 5mph, even including the countless times I stopped to measure my Chasing Ducks distances. I have to say I got far more out of Chasing Dogs than I did out of Chasing Ducks. The ultimate game, however, would be to get a dog to chase me while I chased a duck. My overly imaginative brain went into meltdown. If anyone ever manages to pull that off, please tell me.

The gently meandering canal kept my mind busy as I admired many beautiful barges while watching spring happen in front of me, the daffodils beginning their full bloom. The towpath ran all the way down to Purton, where I decided to move over to the bank of the River Severn a few yards away on the other side of a small embankment. As I bashed through some of the undergrowth, getting stung by nettles and thorned by brambles, for the first time I actually felt like a Roman warrior, forging his way through the jungle in search of gold. As I broke clear of the nettle trap I happened upon a very old shipwreck, half stuck in the mud, half rotting away.

'The Romans were here!' I shouted a little loudly. Fifty metres further along was yet another shipwreck.

'There must have been an invasion!' I told Little Flying Cow, my mind in full on make-believe land of Vikings and warriors.

Further on there was another ship and then another one. There must have been 20 or so all dotted along in various forms of decay.

'A war. There must have been a battle of some sorts here!' I couldn't wait to discover what had really happened and jumped online to search the history.

Sometimes, you really shouldn't find out the truth, especially if the dream is way better. If only I knew when to stay in la-la land. To my disappointment I discovered there wasn't a Roman battle along the Severn at all. Far from it, in fact. These ships and barges were nothing but retired vessels, plonked here as riverbank defence to stop erosion some 50 years ago. There are supposedly nearly 70 boats, some now long gone with the tide, or packed deep into the shoreline. I stood there, disappointed at the lack of bloodshed along the banks, then turned left, back onto the canal path and headed for Sharpness to find some lunch.

The River Severn is a wonderful place to live and the people who live on it are very patriotic about it. It is, after all, Britain's longest river. At 220 miles long, it's five miles longer than the Thames; a fact that many of the west country folk I've met love to brag about. Kind of like giving two fingers to the city folk. I do love a bit of geographical banter.

One of the most patriotic Severners (not sure that's their official title) is my mate Kev who decided to swim the River Severn. He really wanted to show how wonderful and clean the river is and how amazing the people who live on its banks are. The amazing people part was, and is, undoubtedly true, however after severe stomach issues (something we both have in common it seems) he had to admit that the river was in fact rather dirty. No more than any other river of its size I guess, but from then on, he kind of focused on the swimming and kindness of strangers part, rather than river cleanliness, or lack thereof. Kev took a month to swim the entire length, a feat no one has since repeated.

My towpath made way for the Severn Way as I ran along the raised flood defence wall towards the silhouetted Severn Bridge that didn't seem to get any closer.

It felt strangely remote running along the Severn, only occasionally coming across a few farmhouses which were down below me. Before they built this flood defence these farmers would have had great views out along the estuary, now sadly, their view was nothing but the side of a grassy hill. That is unless the houses only arrived after the building of the defence, which I guess was more likely. Still it was a picturesque part of the country.

It was nightfall by the time I eventually reached the Severn Bridge. Luckily there was a garage just before the start which allowed me to refuel on milkshakes and 99p oak-cakes. My legs were knackered. My quick calculation suggested I had run just over 40 miles already, and still had a few miles to go – the biggest running day of my life.

The first half of the bridge was surprisingly uphill. Bridges always seem flat when you drive over them but it was quite a struggle making my way to the middle before the downhill began. Almost exactly as I reached the halfway point, the lovely dry day I had been enjoying abruptly made way for one of those famous April showers.

'Welcome to Wales,' said Little Flying Cow sarcastically.

Far in the distance I heard some chanting. Matt was standing in the pouring rain, right at the end of the bridge, silhouetted by a streetlamp, singing a Welsh song holding up a flag – a Welsh football team's flag I presumed. It was without a doubt the most bass-ass reception I've ever had when arriving in Wales, far better than the usually grumpy toll-booth attendant demanding £6.50 from me. I do love that you are only charged one way on the bridge – it costs you to get into Wales but it's free to leave. You can draw your own conclusions out of that one.

'Conway! Conway! Conway! Welcome to Wales boyo. Let's drink,' sang Matt who was joined by his dog Lemmy, named after Matt's favourite rock star.

'Thanks boyo. This is by far the most effort I've ever made to get a pint.'

'Well let's get going then. We got some catching up to do.'

'Great. Where's the pub?'

'About a mile down the road mind. Can you manage? You want a piggy back?' laughed Matt.

A bloody mile was actually quite a long way for me after over 40 miles already but I hobbled along until we eventually reached the quiet little village pub.

'Righto. A double Southern Comfort and a Guinness for this man and I'll have the same,' said Matt to the friendly landlord, who looked a little star-struck.

'Excuse me,' asked the landlord when Matt went to the loo, 'Is he that Pritchard fella off of the telly, that *Dirty Sanchez* show and all?'

'Yes it is,' I said.

'I thought so. I best tell the wife I'll be home late with him around. This could be wild?' he asked with nervous excitement.

Matt gets that all the time. Even though his show was on ten years ago, and he is now in his forties, and not to mention he holds the world record for the most half Ironmans done in a row, people still expect him to be that crazy chap off the telly.

I'm not sure how the Landlord thought we were going to make this a wild one. This was a sleepy hollow pub and we were both hoping to be crashing for the night in the pub garden later. Matt had brought his tent.

'Right boyo. Here's another one. You need the calories,' Matt said as he bought me another Guinness and a glass of whisky. It was getting near closing time so at least I had my get out of jail card.

Just then, a dog came into the pub that looked exactly like Echo. Then to my amazement I saw Jez coming through the door.

'Hey mate. I've been following your tracker and thought I'd come and find you again.'

'Right. Another round then!' shouted Matt as he jumped up to the bar.

Eventually closing time came around. We tentatively enquired about sleeping in the garden, but the landlord said we should stay for another and he'd join us. Dammit. There goes my get out of jail card.

That was all Matt needed to hear, and before we knew it there was a bunch of us at the table, drinking our livers to death. Every hour we asked the landlord about sleeping in the garden, but every time he suggested we stay a little longer. 1am, 2am and 3am all came and went and we were still going strong.

Eventually at 3.30am the landlord stood up and announced:

'Chaps. I had better go home. We have a new born baby and my wife is going to kill me.' He laughed.

'No worries mate. We'll head into the garden if that's OK?'

'No, don't worry. You guys can crash here on the floor. It's raining out.

'Seriously? You're a legend. Thanks mate!' we exclaimed.

'Oh, and also here's a piece of paper. Feel free to carry on drinking, just write down what you drink on here and sort us out in the morning. Is 9am OK for bacon butties?'

'Yesssss!' shouted Matt as he jumped over the bar, literally, and poured a pint of Guinness into a wine glass, because he could, and then wrote down the price of a half pint on the piece of paper. This was going to be a messy night.

The last thing I remember was the sun coming up at around 5.30am and deciding we should probably get some sleep as I needed to be in Bristol that day, which was well over a marathon away.

As the room was spinning around I couldn't help but chuckle to myself. Only Matt could have found the world's best lock in.

'Conway! Conway! Where is Conway?' I heard Matt singing. How was he so chirpy at 8am?

'There he is. Come on drink up,' he said as he planted a double Southern Comfort in front of me. I really hope they do liver transplants on the NHS.

By 9am we had settled our ridiculous bill with the landlord, who looked exactly like he had just been given the world biggest bollocking by his wife. Then, with our heads hung low and heavy feet all five of us – myself, Matt, Jez, Echo and Lemmy – headed out the door and back toward the bridge. My head was bursting with every step. It had been the most battering and expensive ten hours of my run to date. Well done Wales, you nearly broke me.

'Sean. Bonjour Sean. It is you. I can't believe it?' said an over excited chap in a French accent waiting at the start of the bridge.

'Hi, yes, hello. I am me.' I said, and in my hungover voice I inadvertently gave emphasis to the end of the sentence which made me sound triumphant about it. Kind of like the way an actor in a play about Julius Caesar would say it. I must have sounded like a right plonka. It was very awkward.

'Amazing. Can I run wiz you? I have hitchhiked all the way from France to run wiz you.'

Did I hear that right? A chap had hitchhiked all the way from France to run with me. And he turns up today, when I am mammothly hungover. Please let him not be a crazy person. Luckily, if there was ever a time where I needed a six-foot-tall, full-body-tattooed Welshman and his rockstar dog running with me, today was that day.

'Of course. We are just running a marathon and taking it easy so feel free.' I replied, still trying to work out if it was possible that I was either dreaming, or still boozed up and seeing things.

'My name is Julien and I follow all your crazy adventures. It's so amazing. When I saw you were doing this run on Facebook I just had to come and find you,' he continued as we all stood there staring at him blankly.

'Wow. I think your adventure to get here is more amazing than my run, Julien.'

'It was crazy to find you. First I go to the wrong bridge this morning, then when I realize I just run in the road and stop two old people and tell them to take me to zis bridge. They looked shocked but said yes and took me here. Now I am here. We run now?'

What a dude. I loved that. Just running into the road and stopping the first car then demanding they take him somewhere, and in a typically British way they just said, 'Yes, ok then,' and went along with it.

'You better not run too fast for us, Julien. We all had a long night.'

'Ah, OK. Is that because you run till late?'

Yes, exactly that, because of all the running. That is all.

We crossed over the bridge and back onto the Severn Way. For the most part we all ran (Jez was cycling) in silence, trying to deal with terrible hangovers and come to terms with the fact a French chap had spent two days hitchhiking from France to run with me.

The miles slipped on by as we stopped in every café – and yes, even a pub for yet another pint – as we headed inland towards Bristol.

It wasn't long before we realized our new French companion was a total legend. He spent most of the morning picking up litter and putting it in his rucksack. It was heart-warming to see and confirmed my philosophy that 99.9999999999 per cent of the world are good, caring people. It's just we only often hear about the 0.0000000001 per cent who are right wallies.

It was the most painful 26 miles of my life before we all eventually arrived in Bristol and settled into yet another pub. Matt sank two pints faster than I could manage a half before he and Lemmy wandered off to the train station to head back to Cardiff. I had booked a hotel days before as I wanted to be fresh in the morning to run with everyone I had invited to join me. By 9pm I said goodbye to Jez and my new friend Julien who was off to find some woodland to camp in. What a dude.

Pritchard nearly killed me

Chapter 15 – Consequences

I arrived at Ashton Court Estate where I had arranged to meet anyone who wanted to run with me, but there was some event going on right in the middle of it. Possibly a park run I guessed. How annoying, I thought. This would make it hard to meet my lot.

'Oh well, you'd better just join the park run then,' said Little Flying Cow.

I wandered over and was about 100 meters from the crowd when they all turned towards me and started clapping and cheering. What? How did they know about me? Surely all these people hadn't come to run with me today. But they had. All 50 or so had woken up early on a Sunday morning to do a lap of the park with me. I was quite overwhelmed and emotional to discover that anyone cared that I'd been busting my ass all these weeks.

It was a wonderful few hours as I met people from all walks of life who seemed to have one thing in common: they had started to use exercise and fitness to make a significant change in their lives and each and every one of them has never looked back. I've always said that if you want to get more out of life start with three simple things: eat better, get fitter, and spend more time outside. All three of those things will happen if you decide to do some sort of physical challenge, whether it be running 10k or cycling across your country. It was wonderfully reassuring to see so many people doing just that and the positive impact it was having on their wellbeing. People are awesome.

It was midday by the time everyone had gone home and there were just two people left. Hitchhiker Julien and another chap called Nathen.

'Hello mate. Do you mind if I run with you today?' asked Nathen. I was quite nervous because he looked like a proper runner.

'Of course, more the merrier. This is Julien. He hitched all the way from France to get here.'

'Wow. Fair play.'

As the three of us headed out of the park I did some quick maths. Today was a half day because it was midday before I was able to start running, so I had 7.5 days to do the 230 odd miles remaining to Land's End, which was more than a marathon a day. It wasn't a completely unrealistic task, but considering I had run nearly 800 miles already without a rest day it was not an easy one. Hopefully, having Nathen-the-real-runner (as I referred to him) and Hitchhiker Julien pacing me would mean I may be able to run a little faster today.

One hour later and I was running so slowly that at times Nathen and Julien were walking next to me on the uphills. My Welsh lock-in still showing its ugly head. I also got lost a few times, for no other reason than forgetting to zoom out to see that my trail was a cul-de-sac, or whatever the footpath version of that is? My brain was still not firing on all cylinders. On one occasion I very nearly decided to illegally cross a train line (in the end I ran a mile further down to cross at an official crossing). I could see the looks on Julien and Nathen's faces, it said: 'How the hell have you made it this far, mate? You seem to know nothing about running or navigation.'

After about two hours Julien must have had enough of being ankle deep in British farmers' fields, interspersed with potential electrocution opportunities, so he decided it was his time to head back to France. It took him another three days before he eventually arrived home. What a true gent. I haven't seen him since, but we still keep in contact regularly. In fact, as I type this, I've just received and email from him about his attempt to break my record for the world's longest triathlon that I set a couple of years ago. It'd be an honour if he broke it and I'm helping him the best I can. He may have very well done it by the time you are reading this. I sure hope so.

Awkward silences seem far more frequent when there are only two of you. Nathen was the first person, other than my friends, to run a sizable distance with me. The odd person had stopped and jogged a little but Nathen was in for the long haul, judging purely by his massive calf muscles. Those bad boys knew how to run.

Nathen was a really interesting chap. He is a personal bodyguard, which explains his badass physique. One of his most high profile gigs was as the Beckhams' bodyguard when they moved back to London from LA. He said David was a just a polite normal chap and very rarely requested personal protection – he would happily put a cap and sunglasses on and do his own thing. I can vouch for this because I once parked my Defender next to his Defender in London and we both happened to return to our cars at the same time. Sounds like I was proper stalking but honestly I wasn't. In fact, I was rather admiring his Land Rover and in particular his choice of standard wheel. I would have thought that Becks, having driven every flash car under the sun in the past, would have gone with some fancy alloys or other but he hadn't. I heard a voice from the back of the truck say 'Nice car mate', referring to my Land Rover, and I realized it was him. There was no airs and graces about him, he was just by himself picking his daughter up from nursery like any other dad.

Posh Spice however needed constant protection, mainly because of the paparazzi. She couldn't even take her kids to school without a mob of around 40 following them. That's got to be a rubbish way to live.

Nathen moved away from celebrity bodyguarding, but he wouldn't disclose who he currently worked for; he just said it was a billionaire who was constantly worried about being kidnapped and held to ransom. What a way to live your life. Is the money/power really worth it?

At lunchtime Nathen had to head off, leaving me alone again as I continued south. The next town on the map was Glastonbury, which as most people are aware, is the hippy capital of the UK because of Glastonbury Festival. That wasn't, however, the main reason I wanted to head there. It was rather because this place in Somerset has a very famous tor. If I'm honest, I didn't actually know what a tor was. I mean, I knew what it looked like but I didn't know that the word 'tor' means is a hill or rocky peak, which is actually pretty bloody obvious now I do know. It's also a popular Scandinavian name too though. I wonder if anyone called Tor lives in Glastonbury? I bet he has to deal with the same jokes every day of his life, especially when he meets new people.

'Hi, my name is Tor. Yes, like the hill.'

'Wow. Were you named after it?'

'No, I'm Norwegian.'

'Is there a Tor like this in Norway?'

'No.'

Silence

Glastonbury Tor (the hill – not the Norwegian) rises over 500ft out of the ground, as if a giant mole had made it 20 million years ago, and has the ruins of an old church at the top. It can be seen from miles around and is quite the spectacle, especially in the early morning when the mist is lying low and all you can see is a floating church 500ft in the air, which if you're a hippy on mushrooms must be mindblowing.

'Dude, the church is like taking off man, it's going to Mars, lets jump on board man and get outa here yo.'

The reason I wanted to get high – geographically, not psychedelically – was that I really wanted to see if I could see Land's End from the top, signifying the home stretch. Well, if you can call 200 miles a home stretch.

It was dark by the time I reached Glasto, and after a pub meal I settled in under a bush just out of town. I wanted to get up early and watch the sunrise so set my alarm for 4.31am. By my calculations I needed to average nearly 30 miles a day from now on to get to Land's End by 4 May. If you had asked me on day one if I thought I'd ever manage to run 30 miles with a 7–10kg rucksack I'd have laughed at you. Now, in the space of a month, I had got to a point where I could hopefully average that distance every day for a week. Isn't the human body amazing? I started to write a text to Mum to say we were on for the fourth, but I quickly realized I was in danger of counting my chickens and annoying the smug gods, so I deleted it straight away and went to sleep.

Death, death, death. That's exactly how I felt. I'm almost certain I was still hungover from Wales and the shorter night's sleep to get up early for sunrise hadn't given me enough time to recover. I packed up my tent, which in the dark was a whole new game as I fumbled around trying to find my ridiculously tiny tent pegs in the long grass.

I also seemed to have a rash all around my belly button. My stupid fanny pack had been pushing the clips from the waist straps of my backpack into my belly, and the salt build up in my shirt had sanded away all the skin. I didn't hurt so much, if anything, but it was looking like it was infected. I knew all too well that a rash untreated and aggravated daily could stay for a while. When I swam Britain I got a small abrasion on my foot on day two and it took over 60 days for the scab to eventually heal. I even gave it a name, it was called Stuart the Scab. I decided to give my rash a name too, just in case he was around for a while. Rupert the Rash. It had a nice ring to it. I seem to call everything Rupert lately. I don't know why.

I reached the top of the Tor just in time and went to the edge to face the rising sun, and hopefully gain new energy for the 200-mile home straight. I stared off as far as I could see into the distance to see if there was any chance that I could spot Land's End, or at least Penzance, but sadly all I saw was a small hill about 20 miles away. Moments later the sun emerged fully over the horizon, waking the world up with its golden glow. I could feel the heat on my face. It felt as beautiful as it looked. Then, as if set on a timer some chanting began from behind me. I jumped up as I had assumed I was the only person up there. I wasn't alone at all. There were a bunch of people standing inside the old church in a circle, holding hands, singing the most wonderful song. I was captivated. All the emotions from the past five weeks flooded over me as I stood there, contemplating life, adventure, pain, challenges and the reasons I put myself through all this suffering. I don't have the answers, I don't think I ever will, but right at that moment it didn't matter at all. With any luck I was a week away from completing a dream that was seven years in the making: to become the first person in history to have swum, cycled and run the length of Britain. It was all too much for my overtired little brain to deal with as I felt myself welling up. I have no idea how long I stood there but when I came around the choir had gone and I was just staring blankly at an old building.

'Hurry up mate. You need to actually move your legs to get to Land's End you know,' shouted Little Flying Cow, bringing me back to reality. Killjoy!

It was way too early for anything to be open in town I so continued on in hope of a service station with a bag full of 99p donuts, a large coffee and some plasters for Rupert.

Today was day 39 and quite a significant day because I was finally turning right, slightly. You would barely notice it on the map, and yet right it still was. Up till now, for the most part, I had been heading south, but today I would slowly bear west to start the journey towards Land's End. It was also the day on which I would hopefully get my third pair of trainers – in Taunton, was the plan.

It was nice to be on the flatlands of Somerset, the last of the easy running before the hills of Devon and Cornwall. I took some back roads and footpaths all the way towards Taunton.

By early afternoon the hills had started and my pace dropped. Unlike Scotland, which has big hills, Devon has really short and sharp ones, the kind where it's way more efficient to walk, and often a lot quicker, on the uphills. The downhills, however, were just painful, there was no way of avoiding it. I could feel my tendons struggling to keep my knee joints in place and felt that with each and every step they could give up and I'd hear the pop of death signifying the end of my run. It didn't help either that I had misjudged a jump earlier in the day, going calf deep into that really disgusting mud that farts when your foot goes in, so I had one soggy foot and one dry one, which inevitably made me run off centre. For an entire 92 minutes that day I contemplated putting my other foot in fart mud to balance myself out, which in hindsight was the least efficient use of my brain-space to date. I'll never get that time back. In fact, the only reason I snapped out of it was when I was mindlessly plodding up a long hill and I heard someone shout from about 30 metres away.

'Sean Conway! Keep going buddy.'

I looked up and saw a cyclist bombing down the hill at I guessed around 30mph, which is pretty darn quick. Within seconds he was about ten metres from me and put his hand out. For a brief moment I though he was going to wave at me, but I soon realized it wasn't a wave at all.

'He's going for the high five!' shouted Little Flying Cow excitedly.

My brain must have gone through an hour's worth of contemplating in those two seconds as he drew ever closer. High fiving a cyclist doing 30mph was bound to end in catastrophe. If we over connected, or if I hit his elbow or something, he'd be flung off the bike and I daren't think what might happen. Even if we connected at the right part of the hand we could both either break a finger or get the worst hands slap known to mankind. I couldn't do it. It would be reckless and irresponsible.

'But imagine if you pulled it off!' encouraged Little Flying Cow.

Dammit, he was right. If we pulled off this high five it would surely be one of the greatest high fives of all time.

'I can't do it. He will crash.'

'Do it, you'll tell this story forever.'

I honestly felt as if I was in the Matrix and everything had frozen while I stood there working out all the cons versus just the one pro.

Then, almost involuntarily I put my hand out and tried as hard as I could to focus on the middle of his palm, which apparently is the wrong thing to do – you're meant to look at the elbow of the other person apparently?

In a split second we were right next to each other and our hands connected.

Slap!

'Waaaahhhhh!' he howled, and for a brief moment I thought it was a howl of pain and he was about to face plant a tree or pile of cow turd. I turned around hesitantly and to my relief saw him punching the air like Rocky did at the top of the step, but with one arm of course. It was a howl of joy. It was the most glorious high five I have ever done. We made the perfect connection; neither of us over committed to the slap, instead instinctively making millions of calculations in our minds as the correct pressure as our palms joined together To this day have never ever experienced another one anywhere near as beautiful. In fact, I may retire from high-fiving all together. It won't get any better than that one.

My elation was quickly erased when I arrived at the worst road in all of Britain, for running on anyway. The A38 towards Taunton at rush hour was lined with trees and bushes that protruded about half a metre into the road. With no hard shoulder it meant that every time a car came, which was about every 20 sends I literally had to squirrel through the brambles into the hedge to avoid being hit. It took me nearly an hour to run 2.5 miles, by which time I realized I was too late to get to Taunton in time for a running shop to be open so figured I'd cut my day short and plan to get there first thing in the morning to get new shoes. As luck would have it there was a pub half a mile down the road – which, let's face it, is quite often the case in Britain, and is one of the reasons I love to explore this wonderful island.

I knew I must have made the turning point from adventure runner to wandering nomad when the entire pub went silent as I walked in the door. Then whispers started as everyone seemed to make up their own stories about me. If only I could hear what they were saying. Some were looking over and smiling while others had more of a 'Is someone going to ask that smelly person to leave please? We're trying to eat our dinner' look on their faces. I'd normally be up for this game of charades, but tonight I just wanted to sit by myself for a few hours and have a pint, because as I've said before, although alcohol doesn't make the pain go away, it does make me care less about it. Luckily, humans nowadays, myself included, have the attention span of about three seconds, so before long everyone had returned to their previous conversations.

At 10pm I was just about to head off when a guy who had been sitting nearby came staggering over and lent on my table with his elbow. (It was on one of those high tables with a barstool, it would have been very weird if he'd come over and leant his elbow on a normal table, although I wouldn't have put it past him.)

'Mate. I know you!' he said.

'Ah. Yes, I'm the running guy,' I replied. He must have seen it on Facebook or something.

'Don't you mean rambler?' he jested, winking at me.

'I guess I do ramble sometimes,' I tried to joke along.

'So tell me. Why do you have your clothes on?' he said, pointing at my groin.

Awkward silence.

'Well because I don't fancy being arrested,' I said, shifting in my seat in the way we all do when we feel uncomfortable, especially when someone points at my groin and laughs – flashbacks to communal showers at school.

'Ha ha. But you've been arrested loads, so why the clothes now?' he continued.

'Excuse me?' I asked, now quite concerned as to why this man thought I should be naked.

'Don't worry. I won't tell anyone.' He then leant in and whispered in my ear in a very creepy way: 'You're the Naked Rambler. Your secret is safe with me.' The smell of vodka was strong with this one.

The Naked Rambler, for those of you who haven't heard of him, is the eccentric Stephen Gough. He is a a committed nudist who believes that everyone should have the freedom to be naked if they want, and there isn't anything offensive about the human body. In 2003/4 he walked the length of Britain with nothing but a rucksack, socks and boots on. He attempted it again in 2005/6 but was arrested when he took all his clothes off on the flight from Southampton to Edinburgh. I wonder if he started undressing in his seat or went to the bathroom and then jumped out and shouted 'Surprise!' I hope the latter.

One of my mates got naked on a flight once. Yes, you guessed it, Matt. On that occasion he also apparently urinated on Dolph Lundgren – and if there's one person in the world you didn't want to pee on . . . Matt didn't get arrested though. Instead he made it onto the Mail Online. I really hope Matt writes a book one day.

Anyway, Mr Gough has since spent a considerable amount of time in and out of prison for being naked. It's also worth noting Stephen is significantly older and way more haggard than I am as well as being 6'4" tall.

'Ha ha. No, mate. I'm not the Naked Rambler. I am way more ginger than he is.' I replied jokingly.

'Sure,' he replied, winked at me again. Just then his elbow slipped off the table and he banged his chin.

'Oops,' he said as he frantically tried to rub away the pain. 'Don't worry. Your secret is safe with me,' he repeated and wandered back to his table, nearly taking out a standard lamp on the way.

I chuckled to myself at the idea that someone really thought I was the chap who wanders around stark bollock naked. I finished up my pint and started out of the door when I suddenly heard drunken man shout out for the whole pub to hear: 'Everybody. Look! It's the Naked Rambler!'

I've never run so fast out of a pub in my entire life.

Julien who hitchhiked from France to run with me

Chapter 16 – The Flying Runner

I made it into Taunton as soon as the shops opened the next morning. I went to check my bank balance to see what shoes I could afford. To my horror I seemed to have really overspent in the previous few weeks. I can only put it down to the four hotels I stayed in when I should have camped instead. I had hoped to get some top of the range running shoes for the last leg but instead I had to go to Sports Direct and get a marked down pair. After trying on a few different shoes, I eventually settled for a pair that cost £39. Although they seemed much better value for comfort than the £130 pair I had on, they certainly didn't feel as secure on my ankles. But with only a week left I hoped they would last. I also managed to get some better plasters and some antiseptic cream for Rupert the Rash, who was now looking pretty disgusting.

Not getting to Taunton the day before to buy shoes as I had planned turned out to be a huge misjudgement, and I blame it entirely on the A38. Instead of trying shoes on when my feet were swollen after a day's running, I tried them on in the morning when they had shrunk back down. An hour out of Taunton and my feet were killing me; my toes felt like grapes on the verge of exploding at the ends of my shoes. This was a disaster. I needed a size bigger but being way over budget already I couldn't justify buying a new pair. I'd just have to suffer away and hope we had a sudden cold spell – snow ideally – to keep my feet from ballooning in the heat.

'Seano! Keep go. . .' is all I heard before the sound of a paramotor drowned out the voice. I knew immediately who it was. I only had one friend who was skilled enough to buzz a few feet above me in a paramotor, Alex Ledger!

He circled up again and pointed to a field ahead, where he could land. I followed him over.

'Mate. You're smashing it. But enough of this land stuff. You need to do Land's End to John O'Groats by air. Come, let's get the basics done, I'll teach you.' Alex is a friend of mine who lives in Chamonix for half the year and out the back of his huge custom campervan the other half. He is a proper go getter and when he has an idea he doesn't piss around. So it made complete sense in his mind that I should do some ground handling right there and then. Ground handling is where you learn how to carry the wing (the parachute bit), unfold it, lay the lines out, lift it off the ground with the wind from the right direction and then stand, much like you would with a kite, and feel how the wing handles in the air. I loved Alex's enthusiasm for when we maybe, potentially, fly the length of Britain at an unknown time in the future – even though I have no idea how to paraglide, let alone paramotor, but I guess today was the day I would find out.

Within seconds I had been strapped into the harness and Alex was launching the wing off the ground, all the while repeating the six checks I always needed to remember before launching a wing. I can only remember one of them now – helmet, always wear a helmet. That was already very much ingrained in me anyway though when I was run over on my bicycle in America, I'm certain wearing my helmet saved me from a more serious injury.

The first gust of wind lifted me off the ground about a foot. It was exhilarating – nearly as much as the previous day's high-five. The second gust took me at least three feet and carried me about six feet away. After the first half second when my brain decided 'Oh well, I'm going to die, which is a real shame because I hadn't sent over the inscription for my new gravestone to anyone yet, and I'll therefore probably be given a pretty boring standard one', was over I was hooked. Being up in the air was strangely uplifting – excuse the pun – and weirdly calming.

'Yes, mate, You're a natural,' shouted Alex excitedly. I could see his brain already planning our length of Britain flight. 'Right, let's go to the other end and see if we can get you to fly ten metres across the field, but keeping low to the ground.'

'Am I ready?'

'Yeah!'

His 'yeah' went up at the end, which made it sound more like a question rather than a statement.

'Right Seano. Here's a good gust. If you're heading too high pull these cords. But don't worry, I've got your back. I've taught hundreds of people how to fly. I'm very good at it.'

With that I was quickly launched a few feet into the air and started moving forward. It felt incredible. After about what I thought was ten metres I heard Alex shout, 'Nice one mate. Pull the cord now.'

I pulled hard and looked down to where I was going to land.

'No, No, Nooooo,' I shouted. Right in my path, in the exact spot where I was going to land, was the world's biggest cow pat. It must have been nearly two feet across. Unfortunately, unlike in the high five situation, life didn't slow down, instead it seemed to speed up. Instinctively I pulled the brake cord even harder in the hope I'd land a metre or so before the cow pat. I dropped back down to earth. It had worked, I was going to land about two metres before the pile of turd. Result!

'Yes!' I shouted as my feet landed perfectly on the soft grass. Feeling smug I pulled the cords down, letting the wing fall forward. However, just as I did so, another gust took the wing as it was nearing the ground and pulled me flat on my face. It was dragging me toward the pile of turd. I turned onto my back to avoid a faceplant just in time, and I felt the warm mush cover the lower part of my back and ooze into my running shorts.

Alex was quite literally rolling on the floor laughing. I stood up to assess the damage. It was carnage. From behind it looked like I'd had the worst case of diarrhoea known to man. It's safe to say my first attempt at paragliding didn't go well at all. I guess paramotoring, when you have an engine strapped to your back, was possibly out of my league.

As a side note, even though I managed to do several flights where I didn't land in cow poo over the next couple of years, I wasn't quite ready for the epic John O'Groats to Land's End flight that Alex organized for a few of our friends. They completed it in a staggering 6.5 days in the summer of 2016. That's pretty inspiring, but not nearly as inspiring as my friend Cayle Royce, a double leg amputee, who did it in a Paratrike, which is basically a three wheeled buggy with a rotor attached to the back, and the wing clipped in to the frame. Cayle is one extraordinary human, who has also rowed across the Atlantic Ocean twice – once with a crew of four people who only had three legs between them.

After saying goodbye to Alex, my route started to turn slightly more east towards the ever-looming Dartmoor. I was excited to get back into the wild after days of back roads and farmland. Certain areas of Dartmoor are also the only parts of England and Wales where you can legally camp wild and I was really looking forward to a guilt-free night in a million-star hotel – well, unless it was cloudy and I couldn't see any of them in the sky. Hopefully it wouldn't be. A good night outdoors is always the best hotel in the world.

I don't know what it is about roads that are rutted deep into the ground that gets all me excitable. I guess it's the image of hundreds of years of use; horse and carts, cattle, flocks of Bagot goats and an army of Roman warriors all carving their way through the British countryside. They're called holloways I believe, or sometimes 'sunken lanes', and there's different theories for how they are made, but it's often simply the years of use that have worn the path or road deep below ground level.

It was around 5pm when I came across the most incredible example of these holloways. It must have been 20 feet below the ground and covered with trees over the top, making it look like I was going into a tunnel. I imagined where I may land up upon entering this huge porthole into the undergrowth, big enough for a large tractor to go inside. Narnia, perhaps, or maybe I'd emerge right in the middle of a Roman fort. I turned to my right and picked a bit of nettle and gently touched it against my thigh. I presumed Roman warriors were a little more aggressive when they applied their nettles, with a right old slap I guessed, but I was still a rookie nettle applicator, and even the slight brush still hurt like Ecclefechan.

The tunnel was no more than 100 meters long but seemed to take forever as my over-imaginative brain wondered and wandered to all sorts of completely unrealistic fairytale worlds, a complete waste of brain space to be honest but I loved it. These were the moments where I thought that actually, maybe I could be a runner one day.

About half an hour later, and sadly nowhere near Narnia, I saw two runners coming towards me and so I did what every runner in the world does and immediately increased my pace slightly, while opening my palms to give me a more powerful style and lifting my chest as if I knew all about this running malarkey.

Annoyingly it was a dead straight road, so I'd have to keep up this ridiculous charade for longer than I'd have wanted to, but fake it till you make it, as they say. As I got closer, I realized they looked rather familiar actually. The one on the right looked exactly like my old business partner, James. Worryingly, my eyes were struggling to focus, a sure sign of fatigue.

'Seano, good work. How's the legs?'

It *was* James and with him was one of my oldest friends from my photography days in London – Jon Chater.

'You may have done some miles mate, but we've driven all the way from London to Devon to run with you for a few hours so you better pick up the pace.'

'My knees are killing me!'

'I bet. Don't worry, my lanky legs don't run so well either,' joked Jon.

'Have you soiled yourself mate?'

'Um, no, I fell in some cow dung while trying to paraglide?' don't ask.'

James and Jon just kind of nodded as if this was a totally normal thing to happen to me. I'm not sure if I want to be that guy, the one where people just expect you to be weird, but it seems I have somehow become that guy amongst my friends, who don't often question anything nowadays, even if it looked like I had soiled myself.

'Right boys, lets hit it.'

Their enthusiasm was infectious and the miles slipped away, only hindered every half an hour by me asking them to slow down. Damn these over-keen rookies.

It was great to have more friendly faces with me and we passed the time chatting about the old days. Jon and I met when I worked in a photographic lab in London. Although the work was dull and the pay rubbish, I still have fond memories of those early years, learning my trade, trying out new photography ideas and scratching my youthful creative itch whenever I could. Developing people's holiday snaps was actually quite interesting, and we even used to develop photos for Kate Moss, Paul McCartney and Ewan McGregor, who had all the girls swooning because he was always riding a motorbike and playing the guitar –though not at the same time, obviously. I worked in that lab for six years, gradually cutting my days down from six a week till eventually I had enough photography clients to quit the lab altogether. The turning point was when I was able to cut down from five to four days a week. Before that, I'd never get two days off in a row, but now I often got Sunday and Monday off, which allowed me two full days to try and get more photography jobs. That's when James and I started to work together and eventually started the School Portrait Photography business, which we called LifePix. If you had a child at nursery school in London, the Midlands or the Channel Islands between 2003 and 2011 then it's likely me or James took the photos of your child that we tried to flog to you.

The early days were great and the only real annoyance was dealing with parents' complaints about the photos. Of all the complaints, you'll never guess one of the most common ones. It was, 'You've made my kid ginger and he's definitely not ginger.' We all used to laugh in the office when we got that one in, and a couple of times I seriously considered sending them a picture of myself to show them who they were emailing. The way we colour graded our photos sometimes made light brown hair look a little 'African Sunset Blonde'. Apart from that we were very good at photographing crying babies. Before long, we were leading the way in our field, with secure online ordering and offering each parent eight different photos as opposed to the two or three our main competition did, at a much lower price.

The business started making so much money and kept us so busy that I very soon started to say no to the more creative photography jobs that came in. That was our biggest mistake, choosing the money over ambition and fulfilment. You can be sure when you earn more money your lifestyle doesn't change all that much, you just buy more expensive versions of the things you have already: you buy a bigger LCD Smart TV, buy a fancier car that you still can't drive faster than 70mph, and order the most expensive bottle of wine on a night out to which your friends give that slight nod while lowering the side of their mouths and lifting their eyebrows as if to say; 'Well done Sean, you must be doing well in life to afford that bottle.' To be honest. I couldn't bloody taste the difference. I don't even like wine all that much I mean yes there are good bottles and bad bottles, like in anything, but when I look back now it seemed ridiculous to spend £50 on a bottle of fermented grapes for peer recognition, and not the appreciation of it. If you love wine, that's a different story – go crazy.

Eventually, after getting to the stage where we were photographing 10,000 snotty-nosed babies per year, all in the same eight poses, against a white background, I became so depressed that soon after my thirtieth birthday I asked James to buy me out of the business. He offered me £1, which I gladly accepted. Overnight I went from being cash rich and time poor to time rich and cash poor, and so began my new life of endurance adventure, being outdoors, training hard, constantly cold, wet, hungry and tired but it's been totally worth it. James stopped doing school portraits too after a while, and is now one of the leading outdoor photographers in the UK. Which is wonderful, but not nearly as wonderful as the fact we are still friends, when things could have very easily gone sour between us.

That night we landed up in a pub and carried on the nostalgia with a steak and a whisky. Life was good again. That night we found a campsite and passed out after a good day in the road. I had done a few more miles than I had planned due to feeling like I needed to run faster to impress friends. This was a nice surprise because I thought my cow pat flying skid would have put me behind schedule. Another reason for my extra miles was my overall good mood which makes me fatigue slower. Remember my fifth and final category for endurance challenges – Mindset. It's probably the most important one.

In the morning James and Jon drove back to London for a shower while I carried on running with cow pat on my shorts. In all the commotion and excitement of paramotoring and being surprised by James and Jon, I hadn't quite paid due attention to my navigation. Annoyingly, it seemed that when Jon and James met me I should have turned south slightly instead of taking the more easterly direction I was now on. This meant that by the end of the day I was already 10 miles North East of Exeter. At some point last night I should have turned left and headed straight to Exeter. This was a real bummer, because in order to run through Dartmoor – which I had my heart set on – I was going to have to go back on myself slightly and head south. In essence I was doing the two sides of a triangle instead of the shorter one had I worked this all out in time. In theory it wasn't really a big deal having to run an extra ten miles, but it annoyed me none the less because it seemed every hour mattered now. As it stood I was likely to only get to Lands End on the 5th May, unless I put in a few 30+ mile days, which would not be easy considering Dartmoor and the hills of Cornwall were in my way.

Begrudgingly I turned back on myself and headed towards Exeter, making the most of the early morning when my feet were not swollen and my shoes actually felt comfortable, which usually only lasted about an hour.

Protein was still my biggest nutritional issue when running. I needed at least 140g per day to aid with my muscle recovery, which is actually quite hard to do. I'd need to eat a 20oz steak every day to get that much protein in me. This was very impractical, not just because of the sheer size of a 20oz steak, but because I'd be bankrupt in no time. Especially as I'm a steak snob. I just can't bring myself to buy rubbish meat. Free range, local, massaged and born to the sound of Mozart is what I'm talking about. That's a real steak.

So I simply couldn't afford to eat fresh protein every day. The volume and expense was just too much. In fact, if you include water, I was consuming my entire body weight every eight days. I needed to be resourceful in how I got protein. In all the adventures I have done over the years, this has become quite the challenge. When I was completing the world's longest triathlon I in 2016 I even resorted to eating dog treats. I found out that, weirdly, some treats have more protein per 100g than steak. I was standing in a supermarket with the dog treats in my hand, when it occurred to me that I should phone the manufacturer to make sure I wouldn't die – or spend a week on the loo. This made for a very interesting phone call:

'Hello, Pedigree Dog Food, how can I help you?'

'Good morning. I'd like to eat some of your beef chews. Will I die?' I said nervously.

'No problem, sir. Please hold,' said the chap in a very calm voice, as if he got that question all the time. Maybe he did. I can't have been the first person that this had occurred to. That made me chuckle.

After about 30 seconds on hold listening to some song by Coldplay, the man came back on the line with something he was obviously reading off a page, probably the FAQ section of the Pedigree website, which I probably could have gone to myself.

'Our dogfood is cooked to a temperature safe for human consumption . . .'

And then his tone changed, and I presumed he was going off script.

'. . . but just don't do it mate!' He burst out laughing.

We had a bit more banter about grams and protein before he had to dash to another customer who was wondering if the deer antler dog chews were actually real deer.

Ignoring the chap's advice, I bought the pack of chews, which only cost £1, and got myself a whopping 35g of protein in the process. I have to admit it tasted dog-damn awful but as a ratio of cost per gram of protein, it was well worth it.

Today's protein options were honesty box eggs. I hadn't seen any honestly boxes with produce in them once, most were empty either because they were sold out, or more likely, because it was winter. As soon as I saw the first beautifully laden box with a stack full of egg boxes my mouth began to water. I don't normally crave raw eggs, or cooked ones either, but the human body is sometimes very good at telling you what it needs. A skill that we all seem to have lost over time, listening to our bodies.

The going rate for six eggs was around £1.50 and each egg has about 6g of protein in it. I found my first batch of eggs a few miles before Exeter and decided I'd only have three of them as breakfast was looming. I figured I'd give £1 for three eggs, because, well, it seemed a fair levy for disrupting the farmers half dozen boxes, all laid out neatly.

I cracked the first egg, put my head back, opened the shell and let the egg flop out, straight down my throat. It was pure precision. The same with the second egg. I was a natural and it was way better than the dog food. If there was Olympic egg swallowing event I'd get gold for sure. High fives and egg swallowing. That's surely the title of my next book.

By the third egg I was getting a little cocky and wondered if I could open the egg with one hand, like I've seen Jamie Oliver do. Nonchalantly I cracked the egg, put my head back and put my thumb and little finger in the right place to open the crack apart. It was going perfectly until right at the point when it was about to open, the egg broke in my hands sending shafts of yoke and egg-white all over my face and, worse of all, right into the heart of my beard.

'Can I help you?'

I looked up to see a lovely old lady. Dammit! How long had she been there? I must have been in zombie mode. Had she seen my egg splattering antics. Probably.

'I'm OK thanks. Just fancied a few eggs of a morning. I paid £1 for three. I hope that's OK?' I asked nervously.

'No problem at all. Take a couple more if you want. We have loads,' she said, all the while staring at the egg dripping off the end of my beard, but saying nothing, much like we all do when we see something in someone's teeth or a chap with his fly down. The look on her face suggested she wanted to vomit at the sight of me. Yet still she was very polite. It was very awkward.

I said my thank yous, took two more eggs, put them in my fanny pack and carried on towards Exeter for breakfast. For the next 1.2 miles bits of egg dripped all over my shirt, my shoes and like Hansel and Gretel, all the way down the road into the middle of Exeter.

I remembered Exeter very well from when I cycled Land's End to John O'Groats, my first ever adventure. Then, I got completely lost on Dartmoor and arrived in Exeter late at night, so I decided to have a night in a youth hostel because there were no campsites nearby, according to my pile of paper maps. This was way before smartphones, and one of my pannier bags was full of maps, guidebooks, lists of campsite and a Lonely Planet. How times have changed.

This is what I wrote in my diary:

As there are no campsites available, I have decided to spend the night in a hostel. I have been put in a dorm of 12 people. It feels really cramped and claustrophobic. There are some real characters here too. At the dining table there are all the traveller egos, telling their best travel tales trying to one-up each other. It's quite amusing as I have heard all these stories a million times over. Really, you would think bringing out the 'Yeah, so I lived in Kathmandu for a month' story is old hat by now. Who hasn't done that? Actually, I haven't. But that's not the point. Loads of people have. Choose a better story mate. Then there is the token Asian chap who can't speak a word of English and just sits in the corner watching TV which he blatantly can't understand yet seems to be glued to. In the lounge are the lads (who must be builders from Eastern Europe) who live in the hostel permanently and look upon us folk as flies encroaching on their cake. Why on earth would you live here? It's not even cheap. Lastly there are the group of 'mature' travellers who, for whatever reason, decide to start travelling in their late fifties. They are the most interesting, and travel to places they want to and not to the places the 'Ego Travellers' go to just to get the stamp in the passport. My favourite was Sophie from Australia.

I asked her where she had been and she started to rattle off all the interesting places she has seen. I was very jealous although took comfort in the fact I still have 25 years to do what she has done by her age.

'Cool!' is all I could say. I just wanted her to carry on but then one of the Ego Travellers butted in, trying to get the one-up on Sophie.

Sophie and I spent the next few hours chatting away. I was glad she was there and I didn't have to spend the entire evening with Ego Travellers.

Must have been midnight by the time I headed up to the dorm after saying goodnight to Sophie and taking her email. It was dark and I couldn't turn the light on. This sucks! I have the top bunk near the window. A huge streetlamp lights up my whole bed. Luckily I am tired and hope to get a good sleep. That is if no one snores!

They bloody snored! All of them. It was like a very bad choir. I hate hostels. Camping is the way forward from now on. People snoring, farting, talking, and worst of all, the guy on the bunk below must have been dreaming about Angelina Jolie all night. There was a lot of groaning! I have to get out of here now! I headed out early and got totally lost again but soon found the A30.

That was the last time I ever stayed in a youth hostel and to this day I have always tried to camp instead – a decision I shall hopefully take to the grave with another note for my gravestone: 'And here he lies, his final and most peaceful campsite.' It sounded poetic. I'm sure my family won't go with my long list of gravestone end notes. It would probably get pretty expensive for what would essentially be a lot of nonsense, however I feel they may go with this one. I sure hope they do!

Exeter was a lot more exciting when I didn't have to share a dorm with loads of snoring men and could just settle in for two more eggs, cooked this time, and a full English (I was saving my fanny pack eggs for a mid-morning snack later on, when the big Devon hills were burning my tired quads).

Dartmoor loomed ahead as butterflies slowly awoke in the depths of my belly. From memory, I already knew I was going to have some serious hills to contend with. First of all I had one straight out of Exeter. My legs had been feeling good for a week or so and I had most definitely forgotten about my other mascot, Wilson the tennis ball. We hadn't been intimate for a while, probably since before my night at home on the boat, but I decided that if there was ever a time to get back in the muscle management game before hitting the moors, now would be it. A good session bumping and grinding Wilson was definitely in order.

I took Wilson out and bent down to put him on the floor, when I heard something crack.

'Nooooooooo!' I knew exactly what it was. The pressure I'd caused by bending over had smashed one of the eggs in my fanny pack. I hesitantly opened the zip.

'Carnage, mate!' laughed Little Flying Cow

There was egg everywhere: all over my charging cable, my plasters, my battery bank, my phone and a £10 note that I hadn't put away in my zip lock wallet.

Annoyed, I kicked Wilson off the road and then immediately ran after him saying how sorry I was – pretty much exactly like Tom Hanks did in the film *Castaway* – and put him back in the side pocket of my rucksack, deciding to postpone our massage date until further notice.

This was not a good start to the dreaded Dartmoor and I was now 6g short of protein – although, I have to be honest, there was a moment when I thought I should lick the inside of my fanny pack so as not to lose the protein, but I decided against it. I'd had my grubby hands in and out of it hundreds of times and who knows what creepy crawly germs were in there now.

That beast of a hill going out of Exeter seemed to take all morning as I climbed up to the top and then all the way down again. I realize it was probably all in the mind, but I thought I could definitely feel the positive effects of all the extra egg protein. I glimpsed my reflection in one of those fisheye mirrors you get opposite people's driveways and I noticed for the first time that I looked like a real runner, almost! My legs looked skinny, but toned, my chest was out and my head held strong. I wasn't hunched over like I had been for weeks at the start to compensate for my backpack.

I climbed up and down all morning, only stopping once to have my last remaining egg before I reached the town of Moretonhampstead. This was where I took the wrong turn on my cycle that made me land up in the Exeter hostel. It's also the town where, on the cycle, I fell in love with coffee. Although I eventually worked out that it wasn't the coffee I was loving, it was in fact the routine of having a cup of coffee. I cycled from Land's End to John O'Groats in April when it was freezing cold and getting my painful backside off Valerie, the name I had given my bike, and into a warm coffee shop was often the best part of my day.

Today I felt exactly the same, even though it wasn't nearly as cold, and I went into the same coffee shop as I had done all those years earlier and bought a large cappuccino and three slices of Victoria sponge cake with my eggy £10 note. The waitress was not impressed, and even less so when I sat in the corner rubbing ointment into Rupert. I reflected that I really needed to work on my café etiquette.

Fuelled by caffeine and cake, my new rocket fuel, I carried on into the heart of Dartmoor ready to conquer it. It was a half marathon before my next food stop, so I put my one headphone in and let the miles slip by. Within half an hour I was out of the treeline and up into the beautiful open moorland with nothing but a few sheep and the sound of wind rushing past my ears to keep me company.

I thought it was a little strange that Mumford and Sons had the sound of stampeding bulls in the background to one of their songs, until a string of 30 ponies darted out of the woodland, crossing the road just yards ahead of me, giving me the fright of my life.

Imagine I hadn't stopped to take that selfie at that ye olde bridge earlier, which took all of ten seconds, I thought to myself. I probably would have been right in their path. Getting killed by a marmalade – yes that's apparently a collective noun for ponies – would make for an embarrassing gravestone endnote.

Dartmoor ponies have been around for thousands of years – apparently there's evidence that shows they may go back 3,500 years, which is just the most wonderful concept. All these years later and they are still wild(ish) and roaming free on the moor, causing havoc with ginger runners. In my next life I'd like to be a Dartmoor pony.

I stood there for what seemed an eternity as I watched the ponies canter together up the hill and eventually out of sight, the Mumford and Sons song still blasting away in my ear. I always listen to music in my right ear and I'm certain I'll be hard of hearing in that ear one day, and be the annoying grumpy goat herder that everyone has to shout at. I can't wait!

By late afternoon I was at a real crossroads – both physically, as there was a fork in the road, and metaphorically. I had completely bonked. I was out of food and water, partly because I had spent most of the afternoon dreaming about what it would actually be like being a Dartmoor Pony that I forgot two of the five elements to endurance challenges.

My current issue was that the nearest town to get food was three miles off course, which at my current stage of fatigue would be an hour longer on the road. I had already done two to three hours as a consequence of my detour through Exeter, so adding another hour would put me nearly half a day behind, considering my body was only able to run solidly for around eight to ten hours before my knees would explode.

Option two was to keep on my current course, which would mean two hours to the next pub, where I'd have to hope they were still serving food. Obviously I couldn't check anything because Dartmoor pretty much has no phone reception anywhere.

I was so tired that it even crossed my mind that I might find some Dartmoor Pony roadkill to tuck into, although I felt guilty straightaway for thinking it. I have nothing against eating horse, or any meat really. I'm not sure where the food/pet line is or who made that line and why. So, even though I would eat horse if I *needed* too, I felt these ponies were too pretty and too rare to become food just because of my inability to plan my lunch stops properly. Other roadkill however I would eat. The last time I ate roadkill was when I was completing the cycle leg of the world's longest triathlon and a legendary cyclist, who used to have the record for cycling around the world, and good friend called Vin Cox, came and joined me for a few hours down in Cornwall. We were cycling along when he suddenly shouted: 'Stop, mate! It's here I think,' and jumped off his bike, letting it fall over and ran into a bush. Moments later he emerged from the undergrowth with the biggest smile on his face and a mallard duck in his hands.

'Look. It still has its eyes which means it's fresh,' he laughed. Apparently the crows get the eyes fairly quickly, so if they are still there and haven't been pecked away, then you have some fresh meat.

That night we had fried mallard duck breast with rice and veg. It really was tasty, although I had just cycled 100 miles so would have found a sheet of cardboard tasty.

I eventually deciding against the three mile detour to get guaranteed food more quickly. Instead I found a stream and filled my belly with two litres of water, hoping to ward off the hunger pains.

It did not work.

By nightfall I could barely walk I was so low on energy. I was struggling to do more than two miles per hour but eventually reached the pub and settled in for some food, which they were thankfully still serving. I had made it most of the way across Dartmoor. The hills and lack of nutrition had certainly taken their toll on my legs, but I wouldn't know how badly until tomorrow. I knew that what I really needed to do was drink 1 litre of water with salt in it and at least two bowls of lasagne, but the idea of eating made me feel sick so I just sipped at a pint of water and tried to force down a burger and chips.

Although I had dreamed about spending the night up in the open moors, in my million-star hotel, I was way too tired, so I quickly found a spot under a tree next to the road and down by a stream, set up my tent and was soon fast asleep.

Cornwall in all its majesty

Chapter 17 – The Final Hobble

I really do need to learn that sleeping next to a river is not nearly as peaceful as I think it will be. I seem to be constantly needing the loo, the rushing water making me want to pee myself, and I have vision of the river coming down in flood and taking me away with it. I hardly slept all night.

I was getting quite good at packing up my tent and did it in a record 12 minutes before the long painful decent into Tavistock in search for breakfast. Yesterday's efforts through Dartmoor had reduced my run to a limping wobble.

I'm not normally an eavesdropper. In fact, I usually try and leave people be, preferring to indulge my own over-imaginative brain, which I have to say, is way more exciting, and the present time seemed always to include warriors and ponies. However, this morning, at a table across from me were an elderly couple, probably in their seventies or maybe even eighties, having the most morbid of conversations. They were both just recalling people who had died.

Most of the people who they mentioned I didn't know, but the conversation went along the lines of this.

'Sue Townsend. She died recently didn't she?'

'Yes, I believe so, also that Joe Cocker chap. I loved him. It's a shame he's gone.'

'Yes, a real shame. Also a shame we lost Robin Williams.'

'Oh yes. I liked him indeed.'

And the list went on. Not even the waitress coming over and commenting on the weather managed to stop them. It wasn't as if they were paying tribute or doing research or anything. It seemed idle chitchat that had gone off on a tangent and they were now trapped in a conversational spiral which had taken the form of brainstorming recent celebrity deaths.

After another half hour, the lady needed to head off and the man, being a gentleman, because most elderly people have manners and all, stood up and walked her to the door.

'Well, I hope we can see each other again,' he said, as he opened the door for her. 'My neighbour thought we would get along, and she was right.'

Was that a date? Wow! I think it was. I mean, he was chivalrous and all, but seriously, he needs to work on his chat. Even I know that listing dead people on your first date is a buzz kill.

'Yes. That would be nice. How about next week, same time?'

What the.. ? She agreed to a second date. How did he pull that one off? I can't believe I'm still single!

As I was leaving town, another jogger came around a corner right next to me, and I jumped out of the way, as if trying to avoid a pile of dog turd.

'Oh gosh, I'm so sorry!' I said, and then wondered why I sounded like Hugh Grant.

'Don't worry,' she laughed and looked up at me with the most amazing blue eyes I have ever seen. She also smelled like spring. I suddenly felt very smelly.

'So, what are you running away from?' I asked, trying to be funny and immediately regretting it. Where on earth had I got that line from? Oh yeah, Alistair from the clan museum back in Fort Augustus. Great. Could she be the future Mrs Conway Hemingway? This would be a great story.

'Um, nothing. Just my morning jog, my new year's resolution to run more has progressed from running a bath!' she joked.

Dammit. She was funny too, and seemed to make the same rubbish jokes that I do.

By now we were running side by side along the same road. I didn't know for how much longer, so I decided I had to act fast to impress her.

'Well, if you're new to running, it's good to know that most people don't eat enough protein.'

What was I talking about? It just came out.

'Really? I do feel stiff after each run. Any tips?'

Yes. I hadn't blown it. I can claw this back, I thought.

'Well, you need up to two grams of protein per kilogram of body weight so I'm guessing you'd need around 110g of protein each day when you're training.

Oh no, I didn't. Did I just guess her weight? Never do that. What is wrong with me? Also protein chat is NOT how you get a girlfriend.

'More like 100g actually,' she said, smiling.

Dammit she was cool. I had insulted her and yet she hadn't run away. Unless she actually was running away and I was in fact chasing her? No, no, we were definitely just running together, definitely. I could still pull this out the bag. Time for the clincher chat up line. Time to really impress her.

'It's actually quite hard to get that amount of protein in your everyday diet. I once ate a pack of dog food to get more protein.' What??? I couldn't control the words coming out of my mouth. What is wrong with me?

'Right! I bet that tasted awful.' She seemed less interested all of a sudden and moved away from me slightly. Dammit. Maybe I was over my Two and a Quarter rule too. This was not going well.

'The dog food was actually quite good and it has 28g of protein per hundred grams, which is way more than chicken of beef you know,' I said, desperately trying to explain. Why had I said that? I hated the dog food. I was just trying to show off, badly.

'Oh, right. Good to know. Anyway, I'm turning off here. Good luck on your travels.' She looked at me strangely, with a look that said,

'Please don't follow me.' And then she turned into a side road and was gone.

I continued on heading perfectly east, reflecting on the clear fact that I am going to be single for ever.

It was nice to back on some of the old thin roads cutting through hedgerows of Devonish farmland. Today was the 1st of May and with any luck I'd make it into Cornwall, my final county and a huge milestone in my adventure.

'I really hope I don't cock this up at the final hurdle,' I kept repeating to myself, as I wished that doing so would make me focus more on the little things that could still end my run, like torn ligaments, twisted ankles, getting run over . . . the list goes on. Until I high-fived that famous Land's End signpost I couldn't afford to take my eye off the ball. Ah, talking of balls. Seeing as I wasn't having much luck with the ladies, I decided to have that postponed date with Wilson. I pulled off the road and proceeded to have the most painful 20 minutes in weeks as Wilson reached places no tennis ball has gone before.

The sweet smell of spring was now in full swing as swathes of wild garlic took over the forest floor. I love wild garlic and take every opportunity to pick it when it's around – although you have to check that some dog hasn't peed on it. In the past, I have made wild garlic and butter steak sauce, wild garlic pesto and once or twice added it to a salad, although it does give it quite the kick. And it's that exact kick which made the warrior wannabe in me decide, as I huffed and puffed up my zillionth hill of the morning, to see how many wild garlic leaves I could fit into my mouth.

I've had many bad ideas in the past but that really was one of the worst, as my mouth burned for the next half hour, despite chugging over a litre of water.

I was just starting to get over my self-inflicted garlic incident (although I couldn't tell how much it had added to my general smelliness – I can't imagine it helped) when I reached the small village of Horsebridge. As you can guess, it has a pretty old bridge. The sign says it was built in 1437, which makes it incredible that it's still around.

The bridge crosses the River Tamar, and on the other side was Cornwall, my final county. I figured I should do a little dance or say a prayer to Sterquilinus or something to help me get to the end. This was it. The final straight. I ran onto the bridge and gave a teeth-clenching roar, hoping it would last all the way across the bridge, like the triumphant warrior I was, taking on Cornwall with all the might in the world. Unfortunately, the bridge was way too long, and my lungs were way too tired so it finished in a short squelch of air, not dissimilar to the sound you get when you let a balloon go before you've managed to tie it up.

Nevertheless, I really was now on my final leg. I could almost smell the painted steel of the Land's End sign. I wonder if I would be allowed to lick it?

I carried on throughout the morning at a good pace, managing to get a good few miles under my belt. The countryside was beautiful and starting to get really green now that I was in the comparatively temperate West Country and early May flowers were starting to blossom.

By early afternoon I reached the village of Minions, on the edge of Bodmin moor, which seem to have taken full advantage of having the same name as the successful cartoon film franchise. There were pictures of Minions everywhere: in café windows, B&B signs and – my favourite – a pile of car tyres painted yellow with eyes, outside the off licence. There was a Minion Heritage Centre too, but disappointingly didn't seem to be based on the history of small yellow people but rather on the town itself. I have no idea what is in that museum because I can find very little about the town of Minions; people don't even know where the name comes from. In fact, 80 per cent of the short paragraph about Minions on the Visit Cornwall website focuses on a scene from a popular British TV show called *Poldark*, which was filmed there. The one really interesting fact I learnt is that it is the highest village in Cornwall, which is of course why I decided to run up to it. Why make life easy for myself?

I bet there is quite a divide in the town on the subject of their association with the little yellow banana-loving movie stars. I imagined the residents' meeting where they were discussing the matter: Margaret the hippy was in favour and brought everyone a toy Minion that says 'Banana' when you press its belly. Bret, the local American who, even after living in Cornwall for 20 years, is still referred to as 'the Foreigner' also loved the idea, while there was almost definitely a grumpy old goat herding shepherd, deaf in one ear, who probably hated the idea, and was very affronted when someone suggested he could paint some of his goats yellow.

There are other towns in Britain that could also jump on the Hollywood bandwagon; most notably Gotham in Nottinghamshire. I can't believe they don't shine a large bat signal into the sky each night. I mean, you really would, wouldn't you? Although I've been told Gotham is pronounced 'GO-tham'. I think they've missed a trick there, but maybe that's why I've never been offered a job as a town's public relations manager.

Although my afternoon had started off well with a pie and tea in Minions, over the next six hours every pub I reached was closed, and by 5pm I had completely bonked again. When I got to the next pub at around 5.20pm it said that they started serving food from 6.15pm I decided to go no further and wait until the kitchen opened. Eventually I was able to order my overpriced microwaved lasagne which took all of four minutes from when I ordered to get to me – scalding hot and slightly burned around the edges. It's better to eat the wrong food than no food, I reminded myself and put aside my pub food snobbery and ordered a second lasagne to make up for lost calories.

My next task was to look for a suitable forest to camp in so opened Google maps then went to satellite view. About five miles ahead was a perfect camp spot. It was near the road but in a thick forest, so I could avoid detection by the wild camping spy drones of course.

Feeling quite excited about my first night in Cornwall I furry danced – a traditional Cornish dance – all the way down the road to the sound of Eminem in my headphones, which I can tell you was a great combination for overall team morale.

Despite having spent 41 days on the road, it seemed I still couldn't do navigation and logistics properly. My wonderful woodland campsite which I had seen on Google maps, was no longer in a forest. In fact, if you were looking for something that was the opposite of a forest, this was it: a ruddy great roundabout. If I had in fact used an OS maps – as they update their maps 10,000 times a day, or something – I would have actually seen the roundabout and made another plan for the night. To make things worse, I had passed loads of places I could have camped but I was now in some sort of odd suburbia where my options were limited.

I looked at the OS app and saw my only real option was a golf course back up the road about half a mile. I hated going back but knew that the golf course was probably flanked by some large trees, that I could camp among – you know, to stop people like me hitting balls off course and through someone's kitchen window.

I would have to get up at 5.30am to avoid being detected by any over keen golfing types who can't hit a ball straight, I decided. My tent, being the lightest in the world and all, probably wouldn't stand up to a golf -ball travelling at 100 miles per hour. Or, if you're Ryan Winther, who has the Guinness World Record for the fasted golf swing, 217.1 miles per hour, which is not that far off the speed of the bullet that comes out of small rifle using Colibri rounds. I know what you're thinking: great pub quiz knowledge. You're welcome.

I blamed my smug furry dancing for jinxing my camping options (well, and the fact I didn't do my due diligence) as I wearily sulked my way back up the road, found some long grass and a bush to tuck myself under next to the golf course, and fell asleep.

My tiredness from the early start to avoid being shot by a bullet-like golf ball turned into frustration as I joined the busy A38. I had to run on this road for a few hours and it was the worst road I had been on so far. On one side there was a cliff and on the other side a small wall, both of which were so close to the road that is was impossible for two cars to pass me without running me over. So for the next hour I had to run on top of the stone wall, which had a three metre drop on the other side, while skirting around reflective bollards placed on top of the wall probably to stop cars constantly crashing into it because the road was so narrow. It took me nearly an hour to do a mile as I kept having to wait ages for a gap in traffic before being able to dash 100 meters getting my elbow clipped by a wing mirror.

Eventually I reached a railway and got off the road and made my way to the station platform in search of over-priced rush-hour coffee and preservative filled muffins – the ones where the sell by date is 200 years from now. As I've said before, though, it's better to eat the wrong thing than nothing. It's amazing what your body can turn into energy.

It was good to be in Cornwall, it's one of my favourite parts of the UK. Tucked away from everywhere, and even though you can get there from London quicker than it would take to do your monthly shopping if you lived in a slightly remote bit of America or Australia, it still feels very far away. There is in fact a big movement to recognize Cornwall as its own Duchy or even country because studies suggest its indigenous inhabitants, along with the Welsh, are genetically different to the rest of England. Plus they make the world's best cider of course. No one can deny, Cornish Cider is mind numbingly moreish – quite literally sometimes.

Indian Queens. What a wonderful name for a village.

It's seems that every big adventure I have done has some connection with Pocahontas. When I cycled around the world I went through the town of Pocahontas in America. When I completed the world's longest triathlon I went through Gravesend in Kent, where Pocahontas is buried, and this little town overlooking the Cornish countryside is rumoured to be named after her too. She was quite the influencer, considering she died at such a young age, around 21 years old.

As I got to the top of the hill that led out of the other end of town, I could almost see Land's End. My heart started to flutter. With any luck I'd arrive the day after tomorrow, the 4th of May. I wasn't sure what I was more excited about: the idea of finishing a gruelling 44 days of solid running, or the fact that for the first time in my life, my plan, the one to finish on the 4 May, was actually going to work out. When I cycled around the world I got run over, putting me in hospital. When I swam the length of Britain I was 2 months delayed due to bad weather and jelly fish. When I tried to run Britain the first time I took an ill-fated selfie. So many things had not quite gone to plan in the past but it seemed that now I was going to make it on time. It had to, because Mum had already packed her suitcase and my sister and a few friends had all booked a hotel for two nights. No time for messing around now.

I continued down the hill in search of the coast. I wanted to do the final straight along the famous South West Coast Path from Perranporth, to reminisce, again, about the first few days when I swam up that coastline.

I also worked out that once I had finished, if I managed to get a lift home with someone, I would save around £60 on the train, which is the same price as a hotel in Perranporth. One more night in a bed and hitchhike home, or camp and get the train. I decided to make the decision when I got there.

By the time I reached Perranporth it had started to rain, which made the decision quite easy. I'd spend my last night in a hotel to freshen up and get a good night's sleep before the hilly South West Coast Path. I'd deal with getting home once I had reached Land's End. Surely someone would be heading back up to Worcester.

I thanked the lovely smoothie lady In Perranporth as she handed me a litre of brown sludge. The menu said this one was called 'The Gladiator' and, as well as appealing to my Roman warrior ambitions, seemed like a better option than the 'Slim Jim', which looked exactly like the algae/swan poo that collects between my boat and the canal wall. Although I love the smell of canals, I wouldn't drink the water. I get the same feeling with herbal teas if I'm honest. They smell amazing but taste rather bland. I've never agreed with them.

It took me half an hour to chug my brown sludge as I wandered around town. I had thought of running with the smoothie in hand, but the South West Coast Path is quite technical in places and falling off the edge of a cliff because my head was tilted back trying to get that last bit of smoothie would be a rubbish way to die. I definitely didn't want that adding to my now lengthy gravestone.

I was just about to leave town when I saw two surfers run past me heading for the waves.

'Come on Sean, you have to at least have one swim in the sea, for old time's sake?' suggested Little Flying Cow.

He was right. I had spent weeks swimming along this coast, it only seemed right that I go for a quick dip. And on the plus side, it'll be a good ice bath too. So, with the decision made I turned around and headed for the beach.

The cold sea air cut into my skinny body as I stripped down to just my shorts. I piled my clothes as close to the waves as possible so that if some scallywag decided to run off with them I could hopefully catch them. My entire life was in that pile and I'd be rather annoyed to have to run the final two days half naked.

The water felt cold as I waded in but not nearly as cold as that river near the bothy in Scotland so I didn't panic as much. Until I was waist deep that is, that's when the biting started. I looked around to see a few surfers covered head to toe in neoprene and the few people on the beach in full winter down jackets. I was the only one silly enough, it seemed, to decide to swim with no clothes on.

'Three. . . two. . . one!' I shouted and dunked my entire body in the water. It completely took my breath away and I went into fight or flight, my Roman warrior instinct kicked in, and I came out the water and shouted:

'Land's End here I come.'

I immediately felt embarrassed as dog walkers and kite flyers looked over at me, questioning my sanity. I slowly walked back to my clothes, put them on and left the beach.

'Yeeehaaaaaa!' I shouted, now that I was alone and could do so guilt free, as I practically sprinted up the first hill out of town. That smoothie and swim combination really did wonders for my tired legs. I felt like I was a proper Roman warrior as I ran all the way up to 300ft, stopping just briefly to look over the valley I had just conquered. I stopped at the top and had a little chuckle to myself. I had been running for 42 days, and now, on the second to last day, I had eventually discovered what I should have been eating all along: blended oats with two bananas, some milk, honey, and a load of peanut butter. Steve did tell me in that hotel room in Strathy it was always going to take me around 50 days to get fit for running Britain, and it seems he was right. It was around about now that I was starting to work things out.

I reached St Ives late afternoon and settled in for my final supper. As I sat on the harbour wall devouring two portions of fish and chips I couldn't help but feel emotional. I was now nearing the end of my run and overlooking the bit of ocean where, two years earlier, I had struggled to get my attempt to swim the length of Britain off the ground, or out of the water, or whatever. Metaphors aside, it had been extremely difficult. Everything was against me on that swim but I hadn't given up, and for 135 days I battled freezing water, huge waves, storms and angry jellyfish. I was now exactly a marathon away from finishing the third and final leg of the world's first length of Britain triathlon. In fact, even the club of people (there isn't a club but there should be) who have both run and cycled the length of this beautiful island is pretty small – the internet suggests only a handful. I felt immensely proud of my achievements and even as I write this I still can't quite believe that I actually managed to pull it off. It seemed way out of the realms of what I thought was personally achievable.

I was just letting my mind wander, thinking about life goals, and pushing yourself, and what it all means when I heard a splotch on my shoe. I looked down. Of course. It was a seagull turd, bringing me quickly back to reality. I was counting my chickens and Sterquilinus was reminding me that I still had a marathon to run tomorrow. It's not over till it's over.

With that I walked back up the hill and found a bush to crawl under for my final night's camping. Something told me it would be the best night's sleep since the start of the run.

It was not my best night's sleep. In the dark I hadn't quite found a flat surface and spent all night sliding down to the bottom of my tent, and then having to do the caterpillar dance to slide back up to the top of it. By 6am, having become a master of the caterpillar (I may even whip it out at the next wedding I go to), I eventually decided to get up and hit the road. There was obviously nowhere open to get food at this time, but I was very excited to find half a Cornish pasty from two days earlier stuffed at the bottom of my rucksack. I remembered nearly throwing it away but deciding that wasting food was not good for the Karma Gods. I was so glad I kept it. It was quite likely that I would get ill from a pie that had been sweltering in my rucksack for a few days, but I didn't care. I reasoned that most food-related stomach issues take at least 12 hours to kick in, and by then I would either be tucked up in a warm bed, or sitting in the back seat of a stranger's car after hitchhiking back home. Either way, I'd have finished my run and it wouldn't matter. (Although it's highly likely that the person giving me the lift would think differently.)

From St Ives I followed the main road climbing high above the sea mist. Being early meant I had the road to myself. Although there was some fog down below, it was the type that usually disappears as soon as the sun gets a bit higher in the sky. The eyrie calm, a stark contrast with the craziness going on in my mind as I kept thinking; 'Was I really going to finish this run?' I thought that at any moment I was going to be woken from my dream still on the radioactive beach in Northern Scotland with the entire run still ahead of me.

Once I reached to top of the moor I turned off the main road towards the formidable South West Coast path. Weaving my way through the prickly undergrowth, dodging cows, and trying to avoid being blown into the ocean all added to the sense of adventure and exploration I craved in life. I let my mind wander for hours as I ran up and down those hills. I couldn't control it and I'd love to write my thoughts down for you but I think I'd have to write a second entire book about it. I shall call it; 'Wonderings of a Wanderer.'

You'd have thought that the last day would be excruciating, after running nearly 1,000 miles and all, although at the time I had no idea what my total mileage was. As it happens, at St Ives, I had run 988 miles and at some point, between there and Land's End, I hit the all-important 1,000 mile mark, but was none the wiser. Knowing the way my life generally works out I probably stopped on the exact mark and went to the loo or something else equally remedial. Nevertheless, after running for 44 days you'd have thought I'd be dead on my feet, however I wasn't. I was still going. Yes, everything hurt, a lot, my knees seemed 100 years old, my toes completely mashed against the end of my small shoes, my right hamstring was so tight I had a permanent hobble, which stayed with me for years after because my body just got used to running that way. Rupert the rash was still devouring my belly-button and the soles of my feet looked like I had spent the last 44 days in a warm bath, all wrinkly, looking as though the slightest touch would disintegrate them, like kitchen towel in a bowl of water. But today's hurt seemed bearable, because I knew that, as long I didn't get blown into the ocean, it'd be all over in a few hours.

With each step I could smell the end, Land's End! I had said it thousands of times over the last 6 weeks, both in conversations with passers-by, and in my mind.

Before I knew it, I had reached Sennen Cove and my heart jumped. There, a few miles ahead, was the end of Britain. My eyes started to well up and I could feel my mouth smiling from ear to ear. This was it. Surely nothing could stop me now? I was moments away from finally completing what I set out to do, I hadn't let injury, fear, snow, hangovers, a detour to Wales, poo emergencies or anything stop me from completing something I thought would be impossible – the world's first length of Britain triathlon. As I stood there, on the edge of the cliffs I wanted to take a selfie but thought imagine I fell off the cliffs here, so close to the end. That would be the most ironic of end notes to my now very large gravestone which would read:

Sean Anthony Conway.
Loved by all who knew him and fairly competent at many things in
life but dodging a marmalade of ponies was not one of them.
You could always smell him coming a mile off.
He loved wild and lonely places and also looked remarkably like a
Highland Coo, although some say he famously instigated a new
war between England and Scotland.
Here he lies, his final and most peaceful campsite, after falling off
a cliff, drinking a smoothie, taking a selfie, just moments before
completing his length of Britain run. . . but at least he had a
postcard of himself.
RIP

Chuckling about my gravestone I joined the main road and to my surprise there were a few runners waiting for me.

'Run, Sean, run!' some of them chanted, bringing me back to reality.

What a welcome. It was incredible to see people coming out to run with me, some familiar faces who had given me a bag of nuts or bought me a chocolate somewhere in the last 44 days. The runners weren't the only people who decided to come and see me in. As I came around the corner towards the final straight the roadside was flanked by people, all cheering and shouting. I still couldn't believe they had made such an effort to come and cheer me on, still convinced they all thought Sean Connery was running Britain.

Everything was in slow motion as I made my way round the side of the buildings before I eventually saw the famous Land's End signpost. I slowed down to a walk, wanting to take everything in and mull over what I had done in the last 6 weeks. In the end I hadn't managed to run my planned marathon a day due to injury and all the other upsets, but I still felt proud that I had run in total

38.5 marathons, despite never having entered an organized marathon race in my life. I had run 1014 miles and gone through 3 pairs of trainers. My longest day had been over 43 miles and my shortest, a mile and a half. But I had done it. I was here, meters from the sign. I could see that everyone was cheering but I couldn't hear them as my mind wandered. I don't know how long I stood there but eventually my legs gave me that last bit of energy and I hobbled up to the post and gave it the high five I had dreamt about for weeks. The cold metal sending cooling waves down my body. It was over. My legs immediately gave in and I sat down on the stone platform and I started to cry.

Many people, young, old, big, small, foreign and local were coming up and congratulating me. I was very emotional when they told me that I'd inspired them to start running and get healthy. This made me so incredibly happy and was all very overwhelming. After about an hour of congratulations and photos at the sign I was just starting to feel smug about my running achievements when I heard Little Flying Cow shout from my rucksack.

'Nice run Sean, but didn't Eddie Izzard run five marathons more than you?'

Overwhelmed with all the support

1014 miles later . . .

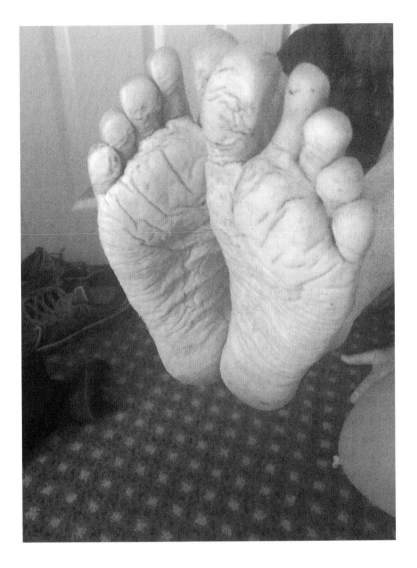

What feet look like after running over 1000 miles

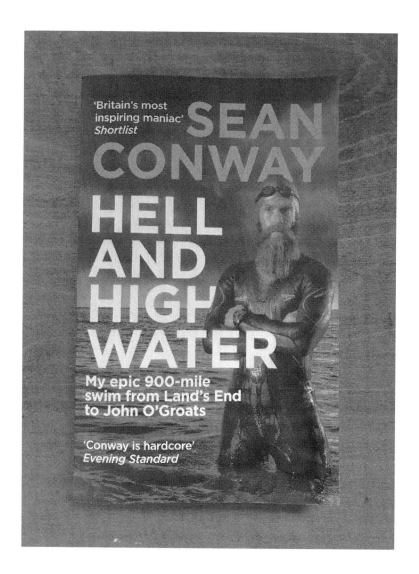

The book about swimming Britain

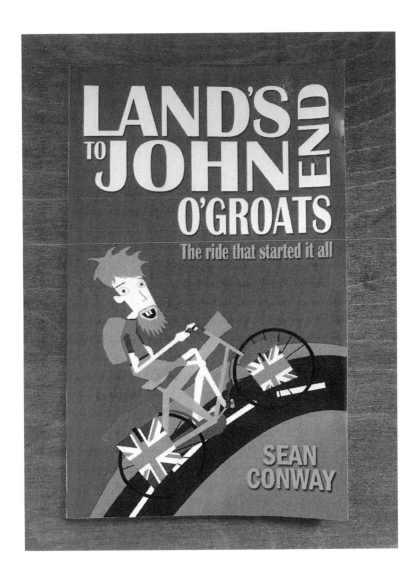

The book about cycling Britain

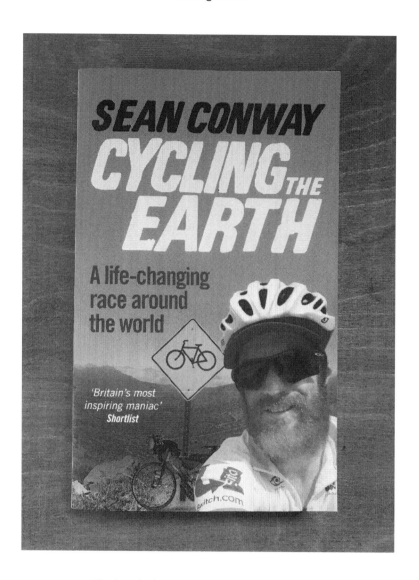

The book about cycling around the world

The Discovery Channel documentary is available on most online platforms. Happy viewing everyone.

31405323R00151

Printed in Great Britain
by Amazon